Make a Living as a Self-Published Author

Richard Lowe

The Writing King

Table of Contents

See books by Richard Lowe at

https://masterofworlds.com

Get free publishing insights and industry updates at

https://thewritingking.substack.com

For ghostwriting and book coaching services see

https://thewritingking.com

Foreword

By Bonnie K.T. Dillabough

Richard has written over 113 books in several categories, but this one was most impressive to me. As with many young people over the years, I remember thinking I would someday like to write the "great American novel". I was enamored with writing. A good friend and I imagined ourselves as famous writers, living in a little flat somewhere with a typewriter and stacks of blank paper (yes, I'm really that old) tapping away as we drank herb tea and having hordes of raving fans.

This is not a book about that fantasy. This is a guide through the reality of a writing career. This isn't a book for hobbyists or dreamers. Writers dream on paper, but in a consistent and organized way. Most books don't sell, and there's a good reason for that. Although anyone can be a published author, not everyone will be a paid published author, making a real living from their work.

If you are serious about becoming a well-known author in your niche or genre, you need to read this book. This book is not a book about how to write. This is a book about how to get paid to write, and therein lies the difference. There are a lot of books about writing out there, but very few that will give you a no-nonsense, soup-to-nuts handbook on how to make a living writing.

This is a book for doers. As I read the advance copy, I was delighted to see the straightforward tone of the book and the practical advice on how to write from the standpoint of someone who makes a living writing. Richard's style is businesslike without being dry or boring. I wish someone had handed me this book when I was younger. I would have been much further along in my goal of getting paid to write.

Thank you, Richard.

Preface

Authors have never had it better. Never in the history of man has it been so easy to get your message–your book–published so that it is available for hundreds, thousands, or even millions of readers to purchase.

You are entering a new era for authors and writers who want to publish a book. The revolution that is occurring as we speak is far more monumental than the invention of the printing press by Johannes Gutenberg in the mid-15th century, and more revolutionary than the invention of the alphabet by the Semitic people thousands of years before Christ.

This is a new age of freedom of expression, in which everyone has the right and ability to publish without going through layers of censorship and barriers to get their message to the public. No longer do you have to face hundreds of rejections from publishers before one takes pity and gives you a chance to publish your work.

Besides a few restrictions on extreme materials, the path is free to publish any original works that you create.

You have an amazing chance to deliver your thoughts, message, and words direct to your audience.

Despite this, there are many who claim that the *Golden Age of Self-Publishing* is over. I've read articles by so-called gurus, saying the bubble has burst, and that it is now even more difficult to get your book noticed and to even make sales; much less make a living.

AI is helping the naysayers even more. They claim that books and ghostwriting are relics of the past. Why buy a book when you can just ask your favorite AI to write one for you?

All this is nonsense.

There has never been a more exciting time for those who want to publish and sell their own works. The potential has just begun to be tapped, and there are phenomenal opportunities for those who will put in the time and effort.

In the past, if you wanted to publish a book, you had to gain the interest of a publishing house, which meant you had to schmooze an agent because there wasn't an easy way to contact the publisher directly.

You could use your own money to print thousands of copies of your book, store them in your garage or closet, and hope to sell a few at local bookstores and get your friends and family to buy a copy out of pity.

Those times are over. Sure, the traditional publishing world still exists, and there is value in getting books published in that manner. Unfortunately, it's just as difficult as it ever was, if not more so, to take advantage of this avenue.

A decade ago, a friend ordered 1,000 copies of his book from a printing company in China. This was a costly move for him. The book was gorgeous, and he used it as a giveaway at his speaking engagements. Except in special circumstances, there's no longer a need for that as print-on-demand platforms such as Amazon, Lulu, and Draft2Digital now dominate the field.

Now you can publish your own books with your message and deliver them rapidly, or better yet, transmit them instantaneously (and directly) to your audience for purchase. You can choose to publish your book electronically, in paperback, hardcover, spiral-bound, and even in audiobook format. You can even create serialized versions to sell them to readers a chapter at a time. These options are available from various vendors, either for free or for a small fee.

This is a brave new world for those who want to become authors. The opportunities are endless, fueled by your imagination and determination.

Don't get discouraged while you are still learning how to write, publish, market, and promote your book to get it in front of your audience. Growing pains are not only natural, but necessary.

Don't worry if your book doesn't sell right away. Take it as an opportunity to review what you've done, fine-tune the message, develop promotional materials, create the perfect book cover, and so forth.

Never stop learning and continually keep updated on how to write and publish, promote and market, and about all the various options available to you.

Avoid the scams that claim that you can learn to write million-dollar bestsellers in a matter of days or even mere hours. Believe me when I tell you that virtually all of them are scams.

Steer clear of the fads or narrowly focused niche subjects and formats touted as the all-too cheap and easy answer for only a few dollars. These inevitably lead to disappointment and don't help you build your long-term career and success.

Avoid the temptation to "jump on the bandwagon before it's too late." [1] Take some quality time to research your market, understand your niche and passion, and build your reputation and credibility in the same way that you would for any other career.

Most of all, don't listen to others pessimistically describing how hard it is to "make it", or that you simply haven't got what it takes. It may be a very subtle message, perhaps even striking below your consciousness, but if you put in the work, get the needed education and keep trying, you may be surprised to find that you succeed.

Don't give your power away to the naysayers or doomsayers. Take their negative efforts as a sign that you are showing true potential and passion.

Start writing today. Get your book finished. Make it as good as you can. Then publish it. The sooner you get moving, the sooner you can build yourself a career that earns you an enjoyable and decent living.

Your book will not be perfect. No matter how many times you proofread it, no matter how many beta readers you find, there will still be errors. A decade later, you'll look back at your first book or two with trepidation. Virtually every author feels this. It's a normal part of the growth process.

The important thing is to get your books finished with the highest quality possible. If you can't afford a proofreader or a copy editor, do it yourself or get a friend to do it for you. But don't delay. Get that book written and published.

---

[1] This is known as FOMO, or the Fear Of Missing Out.

Good luck and welcome to the awesome new world of self-publishing.

Introduction

You can absolutely make a good living as a self-published author. With dedication, it is completely possible to quit your day job and become a full-time, well-established, respected, money-making writer and publisher of your own work.

How do I know this? Because that is exactly what I did.

My passion for writing started when I was young. At seven, I found *Stranger in a Strange Land* by Robert A. Heinlein in a box of books given to me when my grandmother passed away. Heinlein's futuristic world fascinated me with its different views of morality and the power of man.

Shortly after, my mother introduced me to the public library, and from that point on I was hopelessly in love with books and the written word. Books became my best friends, and I decided at that wee age I was going to be an author when I grew up.

I developed a dream early on to write books that would educate, entertain, and help people. As I grew older, well-meaning but misguided teachers and the barriers of the traditional publishing world discouraged me. I also faced the practical need to earn a living, move out of my parents' house, and eventually support a family. I am sure you can relate.

The pressure to play it safe kept me from fulfilling that lifelong passion. I tried to keep the dream alive by writing on lunch breaks and in the evenings, squeezing out a few minutes here and there, but it did not work. Over the years I grew increasingly frustrated and angry at working for corporate America, however well-paying, safe, or pleasant the job might be.

If anything has become obvious, especially in this age of artificial intelligence, corporate America doesn't give a crap about any of us.

Do not get me wrong, I made good coin, a six-figure salary in fact, and the workplace was fine most of the time, but it did not inspire higher thoughts or ideas.

I had all but given up on the dream of creating art with words and expected to go to my grave without taking a single step in that direction. Giving up on a lifetime desire felt like a kind of death. I was lucky to realize that before it was too late.

As a creative person, I realized how stifling my environment was, and I knew it was time to unleash a voice that had been suppressed for decades. So, one day, two months before my 53rd birthday, after 20 years in that job, I gave notice, moved to Florida, and set out to pursue my dream with everything I had. That was the beginning of my journey to becoming a full-time, professional, self-published author and premium ghostwriter.

I felt as if I had come back from the edge of a precipice, and the fresh energy invigorated my spirit. Fortunately, I had worked long enough at a well-paying job to have the resources to take the plunge without immediate survival worries.

Pursue your dreams, but be practical, make ends meet, keep a day job if you must, work part time, sell on eBay, or do whatever you need until you have stability. Just leave time every day to write and promote your work.

Can you believe that decision came only three years before I sat down to write this book about our shared lifelong mission? In those three years I published and ghostwrote over 113 books, including 53+ as ghostwriter [2], ghost-blogged over 100 articles, and helped dozens of businesses with their website copy. The bonus is that it will not be long until I break six figures in annual income.

How I achieved this is a story I will share in this book. I took more than a hundred writing courses, mostly online, read dozens of books, poured over hundreds of PDFs, studied dozens of case studies, and attended more webinars than I care to remember. That work helped build my career, but even after all that I could not find the information I needed most: how to build and sustain a career as a self-published author.

I was not looking for get-rich-quick schemes or "write a book in three minutes" garbage. I wanted to create an actual career.

The average self-published author sells only a dozen copies to family and friends. Do not let that discourage you. That is how many businesses start. Making money requires effort, time, and resources. Writing and publishing are only part of the job. Books must be promoted, authors must learn their trade, and networking is essential to find people who will help.

Do not despair. Many good people will mentor and coach you to gain the skills you need.

What should an author do?

---

[2] Today, in 2025, I recently completed ghostwriting my 55th book, a memoir for an ex-professional athlete.

If you have not written a book yet, start today and make no excuses.

If you are working on a book, finish it, proofread it, and publish it.

If you have already published one or two, promote them, then write and publish more.

Do you want to quit your job and make a living as a self-published author? If so, get busy. Treat this like a business; do the work; do the networking; then write, write, and write some more.

Knock off self-doubt and anxiety. Learn from your mistakes. You will make many. Use the experience you gain to sharpen your skills with focused education and training.

You can make a living as a self-published author. The time to get started is now.

Introduction to the 2026 Edition

People have been declaring the golden age of self-publishing over since about 2013. They\'ve been wrong every year since. The tools are better now than they were when the first edition of this book came out in 2017. The platforms are more mature. The distribution options are wider. AI has made research, brainstorming, and editing faster. Audiobooks have gone mainstream. KDP now handles Kindle, paperback, hardcover, and audio in one dashboard. Draft2Digital gets your books into every major retailer outside Amazon with a single upload. A solo author in 2026 has infrastructure that a mid-size traditional publisher would have envied ten years ago.

The noise is louder too. More books published every day, more courses promising to shortcut the work, more AI-generated content flooding the stores. That\'s real. But here\'s what the doomsayers miss: noise benefits authors who produce quality work consistently. When the average book is worse, a good book stands out more. When readers are burned by AI-generated garbage, they get better at recognizing the real thing. The bar for what counts as a professional, credible, worth-buying book hasn\'t gone up as fast as the number of bad books has.

What\'s changed since 2017 in practical terms: AI is a legitimate research and editing assistant if you use it honestly and don\'t let it write your book for you. Audiobooks are now a serious revenue stream, not an afterthought. Subscription platforms like Substack and Patreon have created direct-to-reader income models that didn\'t exist at scale when this book was first written. Traditional publishing has continued consolidating, making the big houses harder to break into and self-publishing a more rational choice for more authors. Social media has splintered into more channels, most of which you don\'t need — but BookTok is genuinely moving books for the right genres.

What hasn\'t changed: the fundamentals in this book. Research your market before you write. Publish consistently. Build a catalog. Treat it like a business. The authors failing in 2026 are failing for the same reasons they were failing in 2017 — wrong topics, inconsistent output, no platform, no patience. The authors succeeding are doing what the succeeding authors were doing in 2017, just with better tools.

This is a good time to be doing this. Better than 2017. The rest of this book tells you how.

Chapter 1: Why Should You Read This Book?

Are you thinking about starting a career by writing your own books?

Are you looking at self-publishing as opposed to traditional publishing?

Are you working on your first book and don't know how to move forward, or have you written several books that never seem to sell?

The world of self-publishing can seem complicated and overwhelming. There are many moving parts, and it is important to understand what is useful and what can be ignored.

Also, there are an extraordinarily large number of voices claiming–no, screaming–that they know exactly how you can make thousands of dollars a day, or six-figure incomes, or become a millionaire, or some other mindless platitude. These glittery, tempting offers add even more confusion to the picture and rarely produce any real or lasting results–if they produce anything at all.

This book guides you through what you need to do to be a self-published author and make an income that can support you and your family. Of course, there are no promises, as the results depend on your skills, abilities, schooling (both past and present), and the amount of effort that you're willing to put in, combined with just a little bit of luck.

If you're looking for a practical map that helps you make sense of all the confusion, then read this book. If you are searching for a quick and easy way to make a buck, you'll be disappointed by what I've written.

In summary, what I'm going to tell you is how to build a long-term career as a self-published author, publisher, and promoter. It's not an easy path, but then neither is becoming a doctor, physical therapist, or musician. A fulfilling career requires work, training, time, and a willingness to do what's necessary.

There are many, many ways to make a living as an author and a writer. This book explains the steps that I have taken to accomplish this goal. There are other methods that may or may not work; however, what I describe in the following pages has the advantage because it has been well-tested by The Writing King.

Good luck, and I hope you enjoy the ride.

This book helps you get started and succeed as a self-published author. This requires more than reading a book–you must get out into the world, both on and off-line, and walk the walk, so to speak.

The exercises following some sections and chapters are designed to get you to do the actions needed to be a professional writer.

If you do these exercises honestly and completely, by the time you finish this book you'll be well on your way.

To begin, get yourself a notebook; anything will do, although one of those loose-leaf three-ring binders would be perfect, and some pens or pencils. Or use an online app to track your progress. You'll need those to complete the exercises. Before diving into how to create a career as a self-published author, I want to spend a few minutes going over something I call "the writing life."

By "the writing life", I'm specifically referring to the lifestyle of a self-published author who is making a prosperous living in that line of work. This differs from the lives of the freelance writer or the copywriter, who answers clients. Instead, in the "self-published writing life", you answer to your readers.

In my mind, one of the best things about being a self-published author is not needing to answer to a client, a boss, or a manager. The people I answer to are the direct purchasers of my products, my books, and related materials.

I worked in a "9-to-5" job (although for my entire career it was closer to 24/7) for my entire adult life until I retired a few years ago. The mythology associated with working a normal job is that you get a steady paycheck, fair reviews from your manager, benefits, and have some stability. There is also a widely held belief that under normal conditions, you can't be fired or terminated without good cause.

In return, you are expected to produce whatever it is you have been hired to create in a reasonable timeframe, with good quality.

The reality is quite different. In virtually every state in the United States, an employee can be fired for any reason (excluding those which fall under protected categories), becoming instantly jobless without notice. Companies do this all the time—larger corporations can lay off tens of thousands of people if their industry changes or when their managers make poor decisions.

Working a "regular" job gives you a steady paycheck, a certain stability, and those all-important benefits—or at least an illusion of safety.

However, you lose a lot of control over your own life by working at a job. You must arrive at work at a prescribed time, take more regimented breaks, receive reviews from someone who doesn't even understand what you're doing for the most part, and more or less do what you're told to.

That's the reality of working a "9-to-5 job". It's not always negative—in fact, it can be pleasant. On the bright side, you get to work with a team of people who can stimulate your sensibilities and expand your horizons, not to mention provide a social milieu of support, and even entertainment.

The writing life is quite different. I work from home, sometimes spending half the day in my pajamas, only dressing up when I need to go out to a networking meeting, give a speech at <u>Toastmasters</u>, watch a movie at the local theater, or go on a date. My normal attire, if I'm not in PJs, is jeans and Hawaiian shirts. During the day, you can find me sitting under a large umbrella next to the pool, happily typing away on my laptop.

For those who have families, the writing life means spending more time at home with the kids and the spouse or significant other. That's one of the huge advantages of this lifestyle, because a "normal" job eats up the most important hours of the day.

For stay-at-home parents or people with disabilities, the writing life can be an excellent way to make a living without having to struggle to find reliable and affordable daycare or a way to get to work every day.

Once a steady income has been established, the feeling of freedom can be incredible. I spend much of my day writing, but the Muses (another word for creative impulses) visit at different times, making it difficult to stick to the schedule that is necessary in a normal job. [3]

Of course, there are downsides, even to the best of things. If you are not careful to establish multiple streams of income, you'll need to scramble for money if something stops selling because of changes in the economy or public taste.

This is a subject we're only going to touch upon lightly in this book: establishing more than one income stream. In my case, I receive money from my self-published books

---

[3] The concept of "creative muses" originates in ancient Greek mythology in the 8th century BCE. Muses were divine goddesses in Greek religion and they served as inspirational sources for science, literature, and art.

and freelance work such as ghostwriting, book coaching, and blogging. I know that sounds like a lot of work, but any of those arenas could cease and it wouldn't dramatically affect my lifestyle.

A strategy that works for books is to write, publish and market as many as you can. Your income will not depend on one or two books; instead, it will be drawn from all of them.

A traditionally published author I interviewed summed it up well: you can work in your pajamas if you want. You can do whatever you want whenever you want — as long as you get your pages in for the day. If the weather is terrible, the worst you have to deal with is walking outside to check on something. That freedom is real. So is the discipline it requires to use it well.

ANYONE CAN PUBLISH A BOOK

These days anyone can publish a book, long or short, about virtually any subject, for little to no cost, other than their precious time. This environment has created the _illusion_ that writing and publishing are trivial, and the field is wide open for making easy money without effort.

This has become even more true because of artificial intelligence.

There are hordes of unscrupulous people and businesses who will claim to know the secret formula, say they have cracked the code, learned how to cast the spells to take advantage of the "easy money" of self-publishing.

They wildly proclaim that you can create books in less than an hour and have three or four of them published and earning money by the end of the day. Naturally, to learn their secrets you must pay a small fee anywhere from $9.95 all the way up to $50,000 (payable in 3 easy payments), or more. [4]

Unfortunately, despite the advice of these so-called experts, making a living as a self-published author is not an easy career. The learning curves are steep, and there are many specialties that you will either need to understand or hire someone to execute for you.

Making a living, which I define as earning at least $60,000 a year, as a self-published author is not a game for the weak of heart. Then again, doing anything of value such as becoming a doctor, firefighter, an astronaut, or composer, requires years of effort, specialized training, and being willing to take the time and spend the money to learn how to do it.

Anyone can publish a book. A professional takes the time to write a quality work that delivers a coherent message, is free of grammar and spelling errors, and is promoted correctly to the right audience. When you take on the role of a professional author, you have a responsibility to yourself and your readers.

By being a professional and acting like one, you'll find that you are treated with respect, your books will sell better, and you will rise above the rest of the pack.

---

[4] While it might seem redundant to repeat the warnings about scams several times in this book, it's important to understand that you will run into them often in your writing career. There are many dishonest people who want to deprive you of your hard-earned money without giving you any real benefit. It's vital that you keep your eyes open and do not waste your money, time and energy on get-rich-quick schemes, regurgitated courses, overpriced products, and even illegal pyramid schemes.

Be a Professional

Writing is a profession, and if you want to establish a career, you should be and act like a professional. This means that you operate in such a way that you respect yourself, and others will respect you.

Some characteristics of a professional are:

- You've made a commitment to succeed.
- You strive to develop and improve your skills.
- You are competent.
- You are honest and have integrity.
- You are accountable for your actions.
- You remain in control.
- You maintain a good image.

Let's look at each of these as they apply to a self-published author.

Commitment and discipline. If you want to be successful as a self-published author, you must make a commitment to yourself that you will do whatever it takes, within the bounds of ethics, to succeed. This means you'll put in the time and effort to do what needs to be done.

For professional writers and self-publishers, this means writing, promoting, marketing, and publishing even when you want to do something else or are "not in the mood."

Improve your skills. Professionals constantly learn about their vocation. Attend courses, read books, find references, learn grammar and spelling, attend critique meetings, and do everything else you can to make yourself a better writer, publisher, marketer, and promoter.

Competence. You get the job done, you're reliable, and if you make a promise, you keep it. As a self-published author, many of your commitments will be to yourself as you set goals and targets, define priorities, and decide what needs to be done. For your own self-esteem, achieve what you set out to do. If you fail, learn from failure and move forward.

Another part of competency is knowing how to use your tools to their best advantage. In the field of writing, you might work on a computer using a word processor. Understand these and your other tools, taking related courses as needed, to become proficient in their use.

Honesty and integrity. You keep your word, and you can be trusted. The promises that you make will be to yourself and are the easiest ones to let slide because no one else will know. It's important for your own self-respect to keep your word and know that you can trust yourself; it's equally important for your credibility to keep your promises, including deadlines, to others.

Accountability. If you make a mistake, admit it, learn from it, and move on. It's the same with success—when you succeed, pat yourself on the back, learn why you succeeded, and then move on to the next thing.

Remain in control. Whatever happens, keep your emotions in check, and don't doubt yourself. You are going to make mistakes; that's a part of life; don't dwell on them. When things get frantic, as when you're publishing your book, or doing lots of promotions, keep your cool and follow your plans and checklists.

Image. This can be a tough one for self-published authors, because they work from home. Sure, you can work in your pajamas, get out of bed when you want, maybe drink a little too much. After all, there's no boss to yell at you.

Well, that's not quite true. When you work from home, you are your own boss and your own employee. Look at yourself from both sides and make two report cards for yourself. As a boss, are you an inspirational leader, an outstanding role model, and an expert in your field? As an employee, are you reliable and productive, agreeable and respectful?

Maintain a professional demeanor. If working in PJs makes it more comfortable and supports productivity, then do so. However, it is important to establish your credibility, so do what it takes to feel professional. And when you go out in public, or have a virtual meeting on Skype, present a polished image.

By being a professional, you will feel better about yourself, and it will be easier for you to meet your aim of making a good income as a self-published author.

GRAMMAR, SPELLING AND STYLE

As a writer, your primary tool is the written word in your language of choice. Because of that, your most important tools are a style manual, a dictionary, a thesaurus, and a grammar handbook.

For English, I recommend *The Chicago Manual of Style, 17th edition*, in hardcover. This book will be invaluable to you as you write and have questions about grammar, writing styles, citations, and anything else related to writing.

Find a good dictionary; not an overly simple one, or a complex, unabridged version. Small dictionaries don't have enough meanings and therefore are confusing and limited. Large, unabridged dictionaries have too many meanings, which can also lead to confusion and overwhelm you.

Finding a good dictionary requires a trip to a bookstore. Grab a few dictionaries and bring them over to a table in the store, and thumb through them. Look up a few words in each one and see if it does what you need.

Purchase one with understandable definitions, good derivations, and whatever else you think you need to help define words. If you use online dictionaries, find one that has good definitions, idioms, and derivations.

Another book that can come in handy is a thesaurus. As you write, you may find you are using the same word repeatedly throughout your text. To make your writing more interesting, use a thesaurus to find other words that fit. You will also expand your vocabulary, which will make you a better writer.

Another often overlooked component of a writing library is a visual dictionary or encyclopedia. These provide visual context for what you're describing. This can help you write rich descriptions. It's much easier to describe an old New

England church if you have a picture than it is if you just make it up out of thin air or from memory.

Finally, a small grammar book is useful, but not essential. I use a book called *The Only Grammar Book You'll Ever Need*, by Susan Thurman. This contains most of the grammatical rules that you'll need, and it's much simpler than the style manual.

It's important that a writer spells correctly and uses proper grammar. Nothing makes you look more unprofessional than misspelled words, improper grammar, and poor style. However, this is tempered because there will always be a mistake or two in your books. Don't beat yourself up if someone finds a grammar or spelling error (or two or three) in a book you've published. The beauty of self-publishing is that you can make corrections and republish at any time.

Exercise–Take a trip to your local library to examine dictionaries, grammar books, and style manuals. Borrow a few (if possible) so you can test them all out for a week or two. Once you've found the books that work for you, buy copies for yourself.

THE HURDLES TO BE OVERCOME

There are three major hurdles to overcome to succeed. In fact, you will need to scale these hurdles repeatedly if you want to make a long-term living in this field. Don't despair, however, as it will become easier each time you go through the process, until eventually you'll forget that you ever thought that it was difficult.

First, you need to research, then write your book and get it ready for publication. Second, you need to publish that book to one or more platforms such as Amazon, iBook, Nook, and so forth. Third, you must build an audience of people who want to buy not just one book, but many books from you. To sell to them, you'll practice public relations, marketing, and promotion.

However, the marketplace is being inundated with thousands of new books published every single day. This is one reason it can be difficult for an author to sell their works. They get lost in the noise.

While it is challenging to write a book, and there is a large learning curve associated with publishing, the real problem faced by most authors, both self-published and traditional, is getting their book in front of their public.

When you self-publish a book, you face a dilemma that is like trying to get people to notice a single snowflake during a raging blizzard.

The quality of your book or the importance of your subject is irrelevant if no one can find it. To sell on Amazon, for example, a book needs to be on the first page or two of search results for any category or search phrase. Most people will not look beyond the first several pages to find what they want.

Don't despair. There is hope for self-published authors.

I've said this before, and I'll say it again. You _can_ make a good living by writing and selling your own books. It is challenging, but the challenge is the same as with any small business attempting to sell its products or services. Products, in this instance books, must be conceptualized, written, edited, proofread, published, promoted, marketed, revised, and so forth.

The key factor is to educate yourself and refine your process in terms of priorities and focus.

You can master all the skills needed to publish your own books. Take each step one at a time, move forward, and don't worry too much about failure. In fact, come to embrace failures because of the lessons that you'll learn from each one.

- Research your niche or category to find a topic, fiction or nonfiction, that is likely to be profitable.
- Write, edit, and proofread your book.
- Build the audience before and after your book has been published.
- Publish your book using Amazon or one of the other publishing services.
- Market and promote yourself and your books to the correct audience.

Once you've mastered each of these steps, you'll be on your way to becoming a successful self-published author.

A well-known traditionally published author I interviewed offered a reality check worth hearing. Her view: when you self-publish, you're one tiny speck in a sea of other self-published authors. Unless you bring something else — a popular blog, a substantial YouTube following, an existing audience — you're not going to immediately stand out. Her advice on the first book: your expectation should be that it's not going to do very well. Just get used to it.

That's not a reason to stop. It's a reason to go in with accurate expectations, write the next book anyway, and keep building the catalog. The authors who make it are the ones who didn't quit after the first book disappointed them.

There is Only So Much Time in a Day

If you try to do everything possible, you will quickly become overwhelmed and accomplish little. As a self-published author, you wear many hats:

- running a business
- accounting
- writing your books
- editing
- proofreading
- producing book covers
- creating a website or blog
- writing promotional copy
- understanding and handling any legal issues

We'll go through all the steps necessary to write, publish and promote a book in the rest of this volume.

There are a lot of steps, a lot of options, and many things that need to get done. It can be very overwhelming, especially when something doesn't work as expected, or takes far longer than expected.

The key is to figure out what you're good at, and what you like to do. For example, many authors enjoy writing but don't know how to use a graphics program and haven't been trained in artistic design, which are skills required for creating a decent book cover.

Don't spend days trying to figure out that cool graphics editing application. It's a better use of your time to find someone who can create your book cover for you.

You can hire a freelancer to perform that task and save yourself time and frustration. There are some excellent book cover artists on websites such as Fiverr.com who will be happy to do good quality work for you for as little as $5.

Another option is to trade services with someone else who's good at something you need but would like some writing done. For example, I've exchanged blog articles for book covers, saving myself the hassle, and helping another author out as well.

As time goes by, build yourself a network of people you can delegate specialized tasks to free up your time and ultimately focus on what you do best.

For example:

- I use a freelance artist on Fiverr.com to create covers for my eBooks, paperbacks, hardcovers, and audiobooks.
- For my coloring books, I've hired half a dozen artists at widely varying costs to draw the coloring pages.
- I've also hired people on Fiverr.com to do my proofreading, editing, promotion, and even the copy for my Amazon book descriptions.

- A graphics artist created my logo and the graphics for my website, and an SEO expert worked on Google and Bing to send traffic my way.

We'll go into the techniques you can use to build a writing network later in this book, as it's critical to your success as a self-published author. The simple fact is that if you want to make a living in this field, or in any field really, you need to work with many experts for mutual support, which can thus improve your ability to get things done efficiently and professionally.

As you proceed through the process of building and maintaining your writing career, you'll find yourself with a plethora of tasks that need to be completed–some small and others much larger.

Devote a portion of your production time every day to writing and publishing. This is because one of the highest priorities of a self-published author is to write a large quantity of books that can be published and put up for sale. To keep that quantity rising, you need to be writing and publishing books consistently and constantly.

To manage all the tasks and to give the chaos some sort of order, create a prioritized to-do list. This will help prevent you from being overwhelmed by the immense number of tasks that pop up all the time, each demanding your immediate attention and action.

I recommend allocating at least 50% of each workday to actively writing and publishing your books. Split the other 50% up based on your other priorities. By doing this, you will continue to write steadily but still get other important tasks completed.

A handy tool for prioritizing tasks is the Eisenhower Matrix.

The Eisenhower Matrix

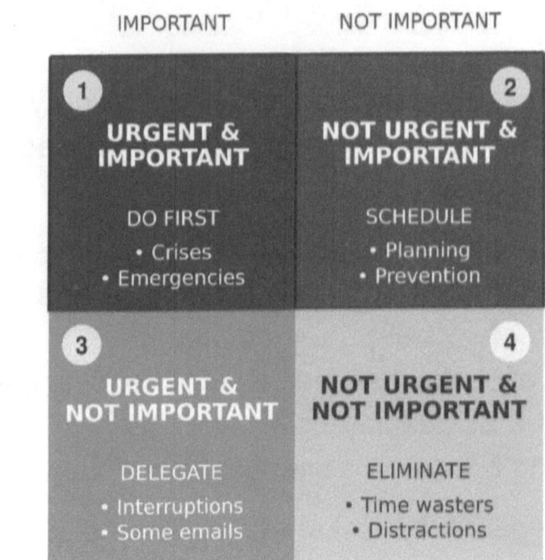

Diagram created with AI assistance from Claude.ai

The Eisenhower Matrix transforms how I approach my writing business tasks. Instead of simply listing everything by importance, I now categorize each task into four distinct quadrants based on urgency and importance.

Quadrant 1 (Do First–Urgent & Important) gets my immediate attention. Writing my own books falls here because it's both urgent for my career momentum and critically important for long-term success. Any paid freelance projects also land in this quadrant since they have deadlines and directly generate income.

Quadrant 2 (Schedule–Important but Not Urgent) contains my promotional tasks. Marketing and promotion are essential for sales, but they don't have the same immediate deadlines as writing projects. This quadrant also includes strategic planning for future books and building author platform elements that will pay off over time.

Quadrant 3 (Delegate–Urgent but Not Important) captures tasks that feel pressing but don't move the needle on my core business. Some social media responses, certain administrative tasks, or responding to non-essential emails might fit here. If I can't delegate them, I handle them quickly without letting them consume prime writing time.

Quadrant 4 (Eliminate–Neither Urgent nor Important) houses those "nice to have" tasks that accumulate over time. For example, adding "this book belongs to" pages to my dozen coloring books would improve them slightly, but it's neither urgent nor crucial to my business success. These tasks get recorded in my three-ring binder system for potential future action, but they don't clutter my active to-do list.

The beauty of this system is that tasks naturally move between quadrants as circumstances change. That book update might jump to Quadrant 2 if I decide to launch a major marketing campaign around the title. Meanwhile, I'm not losing track of these lower-priority items–they're safely documented and will surface when they become relevant.

Using online applications with the Eisenhower Matrix built in makes this even more powerful, since tasks can automatically shift between quadrants and you can set reminders for when Quadrant 4 items might need reevaluation.

Once I've accumulated several related tasks, I may block out some time to get through them all.

For example, my list for book creation includes.

- creating the title page
- adding the copyright notice
- including a short, half-page story of why the book was written
- republishing the books with the new material

Since there were now several tasks that could be worked on simultaneously, I blocked out several hours and powered through all of them in a single sitting. This used my time far more effectively than trying to do them individually.

Every day, I make it a point to reach down into my low-priority task book and complete at least one of them. Sometimes they take only a few minutes, and sometimes they require as much as an hour. It gives me an added feeling of accomplishment to get some of these "nice to have" items completed regularly.

Exercise–Get a piece of paper and write, off the top of your head, 10 things that you need to do to get your book written, published and promoted. Place the on the Eisenhower Matrix, then prioritize each item within each quadrant numbering from one, the highest priority, to 10, the lowest priority.

It's important as you develop throughout your writing career, to set goals so you have a good idea of where you're going. Once you set a goal, you can define the tasks (and sub-tasks) that you need to do to achieve it.

Goals allow you to differentiate tasks based upon whether they help you reach the target or not.

The best goals are SMART, which stands for Specific, Measurable, Achievable, Realistic and Time-bound.

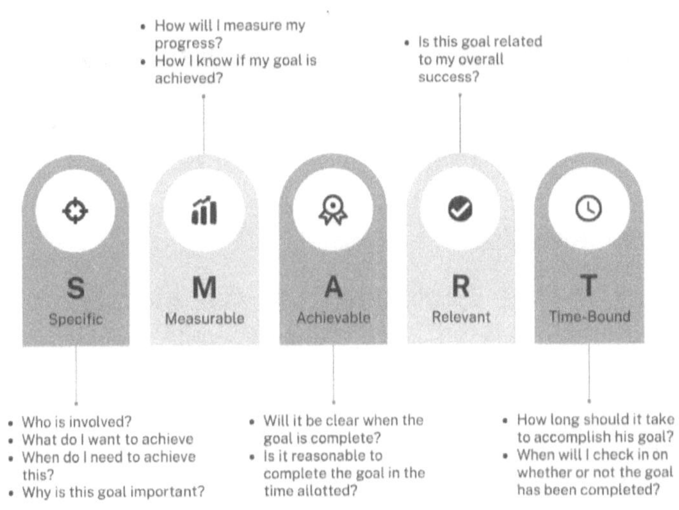

AI image generated by Canva

Specific–Goals need to be specific and not general. For example, instead of saying, "complete writing a book by the end of the month," define your goal as, "Complete the first draft of the book *How to Peel Potatoes* by the first of January."

Measurable–They should also be something that you can see in the physical universe or measure; They need to be concrete and not abstract. "Complete the writing of a specific book within a month" is a great goal. "Becoming more knowledgeable about computer security," is not a good goal because it can't be measured.

Achievable–You need to make sure that they are achievable, considering all the other things that you need to do during that time. Remember to factor in life and living; for example, if you need to spend two hours a day bringing the kids to and from school, and another two hours cooking, make sure your target date takes that into account.

Realistic–Set realistic goals that you can accomplish. If you consistently set targets that you never meet, you'll become frustrated.

Time Bound–Goals should always include a completion date because otherwise they float into the future and may never get done.

For example, if your goal is to get a book called *How to Peel Potatoes* published by the end of the month, then you can define the tasks needed to reach the goal.

Your tasks might include writing the book, getting it proofread, having somebody else read it, creating the cover, publishing it, and doing the appropriate promotional steps.

Exercise–Set a SMART goal for how many words you are going to write for the day, then write that many words. Did you set your goal too high? Too low? Or was it just right? Did distractions get in your way? Make a note of all the things that prevented you from meeting the goal. What can you do about them?

THE DISTRACTIONS

Throughout your day, you'll find there are many distractions that chip away at your time and reduce your productivity. It's vital to your success as a self-employed person to identify and eliminate these distractions as much as you can. Otherwise, you'll get to the end of each day with little accomplished, wondering where the hours went.

Writing and answering emails that have no business purpose, chatting on the phone, talking with people who stop by, and social media are some things that will drain your time. These interruptions taken individually may be small and harmless, but when taken together as a whole, they can dramatically affect your productivity throughout the day.

Social media such as Facebook will totally eat away at your precious time and attention to annihilate the best laid plans to complete your tasks. Many people install social media applications on all their devices, and allow all notifications, so that these devices will be continually pinging, beeping, or flashing.

The Facebook wall can be especially distracting to a writer, especially when facing writer's block. Virtually all postings are utterly unimportant.

Then there is the distraction of solitude. Sitting in a chair most of the day, staring at a computer screen makes me crave contact with people, even though I am a bit of a loner and introverted. Thus, when the opportunity to chat or talk with someone arises, I welcome it. This helps me relax.

Schedule social media and social interaction at specific times of the day and limit those activities to a set amount of time. For example, my habit is to use social media for half an hour each morning as soon as I get up, and half an hour each evening just before going to bed.

Exercise–Look over your space. Do you have a private place, a sanctuary of sorts, where you can write in peace? Look for a room with a good desk, chair and without a television, video games, or other distractions. Set this space up, as best you can, as your office and make sure you have everything you need close at hand.

PROFESSION OR HOBBY?

To make a steady income writing, you must treat it like you would in any other profession. You need to put in the time and effort to make it happen because books don't normally just sell themselves.

Treat your writing career seriously. This means treating it as a business, with all that implies. For example, you'll need to be concerned with paying taxes, keeping your accounting up-to-date, and even small and tedious things such as ensuring you have a local business license to legally work out of your home.

Hobbies, even if they make a little money, don't require that much effort. Making a living requires you to ensure the basics are being handled on a day-to-day basis.

Word Count Goals

We'll go into much more detail about this later in this book, but it should be obvious that writers need to write.

The method you use to do so is not relevant–the important thing is that you write, and you write as much as you can.

I prefer to dictate directly into Microsoft Word, because I have found this improves my speed threefold. You may type on a computer or tablet, dictate into a recording on your cell phone, or even handwrite your manuscript. Find the method that works best for you.

Create a schedule for writing and stick to it. Make it known to your family and friends that you are not to be disturbed while you're writing for any reason except dire emergencies. Turn off the cell phone, stay away from Facebook, don't answer emails, eliminate Internet interruptions, ensure the TV is turned off or, better yet, in a different room, and spend your time writing and doing nothing else.

Another good idea is to set a word or page count goal. Keep in mind that you must perform all the other tasks associated with your self-publishing career, such as promotion, public speaking, book signings, and so forth. Be sure your goals are not so aggressive that you can't accomplish these other tasks.

Don't set unchallenging goals but also don't set yourself up for failure by setting your targets so high that you can't reach them consistently. Constantly failing is not good for one's self-esteem.

PUBLISH

If you're going to self-publish, you must learn to publish. There are many ways to self-publish. Some of them, such as Amazon's KDP (Kindle and Paperback), Lulu, and Draft2Digital, let you publish your books without charge. Learn how to do these publishing steps yourself. Once you've gone through the process a few times, it becomes simple and straightforward.

There are companies that will charge you a fee to publish your book for you. They often bundle many other services such as promotion, marketing, formatting, and so forth into the package to make it appear more attractive. Get and verify references (call them), and search for reviews online to get an idea of how they have performed in the past. While many of these companies are honest, some will underperform and overprice their products.

There is no reason you can't perform the publishing steps yourself. It can be challenging, especially the first or second time through, but if you do it yourself, you'll be able to make changes later without having to call someone else to do it for you.

Before you undertake publishing your book, get it proofread by someone else, preferably a professional. Any time you make any significant changes, get it proofread again.

You'll also need a book cover, the metadata (information that describes or provides information about other data), and people who will review your book for a free copy. It's best to get a commitment of at least a dozen people to write a review within a week of the publication date of your book.

I know that seems like a lot of steps, but after the first few times through the process, you'll find it gets easier. Sometimes the problem is that there are a lot of small steps, as opposed to a few large ones. To simplify, create a checklist of everything that you need to do to get a book published in the order that it needs to be done.

Maintain a Blog

If you're going to be a professional author, you must create and maintain a blog. This is because you need a place on the web that you can call your home, where all the information about you and your books is centralized.

By doing this, you can inform people from within your email signature, business cards, contracts, your books, and elsewhere where to find more information about you, where to sign up for your email list, and how to contact you.

Having a blog makes this simple: you just tell them to go to your blog.

Build an Email List

One of your primary intentions as you move forward should be to get people to sign up for your email list. This allows you to send out notifications to a dedicated group of fans whenever you'd like. By owning and maintaining an email list, you will increase your profits and keep your fan base engaged.

If you don't actively build and maintain your email list, you are leaving money on the table.

SOCIAL MEDIA

Many people are tempted to use social media as their primary promotional method. After all, it seems so easy to post all about your brand new book and why it's the best thing since sliced bread.

The problem with using social media is that it is usually used incorrectly. Social media is a great way to build relationships with your readers, which will, over time, lead to improved sales. Just remember it's not a sales tool and shouldn't be used that way.

Avoid the "buy my book" kind of advertisement or post to your social media. These are ineffective and push away your readers. Instead, write brief articles or paragraphs of interest to your audience, and then just mention your book casually or include a link in your tagline.

Social media must be a part of your daily routine, and it needs to be done correctly to be effective. Executed incorrectly, all it will accomplish will alienate readers and take up valuable time with no results.

PROMOTE AND MARKET

One of the big truths about creating a product of any kind—and it's especially true about self-published books—is that they don't sell themselves. This often comes as a surprise to many new authors who spend months, or even years, writing a masterpiece only to find that they sell a dozen copies to their friends and family…and that's it.

The problem is simple: no promotion. This is a very large subject, and entire courses and volumes of books have been written about it. If you don't promote your books, they won't sell.

Promotion can be as simple as posting articles about the subject of the book to your social media, or as complex as buying ads in newspapers, newsletters, and on the web.

We'll be discussing promotion and marketing in much more detail throughout this book.

Outsource

There are many moving parts involved in creating a published book. You must write it, edit and proofread the manuscript, market and promote yourself and your books, maintain a blog, create book covers, write book descriptions, and so forth.

That's a lot of tasks to perform, and you probably don't have the skills or time to do them all yourself.

That's where a concept called outsourcing comes into play. This is the ability to use other people to do some of the work for you.

For example, visit a site called Fiverr.com and you'll find contractors who will do tasks such as designing a book cover, writing an Amazon book description, designing a webpage, or even writing a press release. On this site, you'll find good rates and talented people to do useful work for you.

Exercise–Visit Fiverr.com and examine the various gigs (offers to do work) that are available. Look for those that might prove helpful to your writing career.

An author I know put it simply: you have one inch to get someone's attention. That's the size of your thumbnail in a search result. She'd seen authors with six books on Amazon and no sales, and when she looked at their covers she couldn't read the title at thumbnail size. The book's interior didn't matter. Nobody was clicking through to find out.

The same author took her cover branding further than most. Her book was yellow, and she wore yellow in every public appearance — yellow earrings, yellow shirt — so that color became associated with her and her work in her readers' minds. That's intentional branding taken seriously. You don't have to go that far, but the point is right: the cover is not just a cover. It's the visual identity of the book across everything you do to promote it. Think about how it will look on social media graphics, in email headers, on a speaking stage slide. Design for all of those, not just for the Amazon page.

LAUNCH TEAMS

One of the most effective networking strategies I've seen is the launch team — a group of people who commit to supporting your book before and during its release. Done right, a launch team handles a significant chunk of your early promotion so you're not doing it alone.

An author I interviewed built a launch team of over 700 people. She started it early in her writing process — before the book was finished — getting people invested and feeling a sense of ownership. She ran themed activities to keep the group engaged and growing: one day was "Add Two Tuesday," where members each brought in two new people by tagging friends with prompts like "tag your favorite person to laugh with." The team grew organically because the engagement was genuine.

Members agreed to purchase a copy, post reviews, and share content across their own social media with a dedicated hashtag. By launch day, hundreds of people were promoting simultaneously — none of them paid, all of them genuinely interested. That's the difference between a launch team and posting in Facebook promotional groups. One involves people who care. The other is noise.

You don't need 700 people. Start with 20 or 30 genuinely interested readers, keep them engaged during the writing process, and give them something to rally around — a hashtag, a theme, a shared purpose. The earlier you start building the team, the more invested they'll be by launch day.

Leveraging Influencers

Beyond your launch team, influencers — people others look up to in your niche — can extend your reach significantly. When someone credible validates your book to their audience, that audience pays attention in a way they never would from a paid ad or a social media post from a stranger. It's borrowed trust, and it works.

The key is finding people whose beliefs, values, and audience align with your book's message — and approaching it as a genuine mutual relationship, not a transaction. You're asking them to put their credibility behind your work. The only sustainable way to do that is to give as well as take: promote their work, refer clients their way, support what they're doing. Networking at this level is reciprocal or it doesn't last.

Start small. You don't need to reach the biggest names in your field. Find people with engaged audiences of a few thousand who cover your topic and reach out with something specific and useful. A genuine connection with ten right people is worth more than a cold request to a hundred wrong ones.

CONCLUSIONS

The rest of this book covers the mechanics of building a writing career — research, writing, publishing, metadata, platform, legal, and money. Running through all of it is one idea you'll see in almost every chapter: the more good books you publish, the better your income gets. Not because volume is inherently virtuous, but because a catalog of well-targeted books is how this business actually works. A single book is a lottery ticket. A catalog is a business. The chapters ahead will show you why, and more importantly, how to build one.

An author I interviewed put both sides of this well. What she loves most about being an author is the autonomy — you're your own boss, you can write in your pajamas downstairs, you set the hours. What she likes least is exactly the same thing: if you want to sleep on the sofa and do nothing, that can happen too. The freedom cuts both ways. You really do need to motivate yourself, because nobody else will.

Chapter 2: What to Write

Before I became a writer, I was a computer security expert and had gone through several specialized training courses on how to keep the bad guys out of computers. This is a subject that I'm passionate about–helping people secure their systems so they don't lose their financial data, their photos, and their hard work.

Because of this passion, I decided my first book was going to tackle how to keep a home computer safe on the Internet. I spent about six months writing that book, carefully reviewing it about a dozen times to make sure it was as perfect as I could make it. I hired an artist to create humorous drawings to lighten the mood, paid a professional to create a book cover, and promoted it everywhere that I could find.

The book sold fewer than 10 copies within a month. By then I'd already published my second book, again on a subject that I was passionate about–surviving disasters. The story was the same with that manuscript–I spent several months researching, writing, and promoting it with very few sales.

I was perplexed but not defeated. After taking a few courses, I realized what was wrong.

I wrote these first two books about my own passions, but I didn't take the time to determine if other people were interested in those subjects.

By then, I had begun working for a company called LinkedIn Makeover. My job was to write LinkedIn profiles for executives and others to showcase their skills and talents. I became passionate about writing these profiles and making sure that my clients were shown in the best possible light on that social media network. I decided this might be a suitable topic for a book and spent some time determining if other people would be interested in the subject.

After about a month of writing, and some good promotion, the book sold over 15,000 copies in its first two months. In fact, it got up to number 43 on the list of top sellers of all Kindle books for a brief time. I missed the screenshot of that amount, but here's the statistics from an hour before.

Product Details

File Size: 2341 KB
Print Length: 147 pages
Simultaneous Device Usage: Unlimited
Publisher: The Writing King (March 12, 2016)
Publication Date: March 12, 2016
Sold by: Amazon Digital Services LLC
Language: English
ASIN: B01CX3B8GG
Text-to-Speech: Enabled
X-Ray: Not Enabled
Word Wise: Enabled
Lending: Enabled
Enhanced Typesetting: Enabled
Amazon Best Sellers Rank: #88 Paid in Kindle Store (See Top 100 Paid in Kindle Store)
    #1 in Kindle Store > Kindle eBooks > Business & Money > Skills > **Business Writing**
    #1 in Kindle Store > Kindle eBooks > Business & Money > Job Hunting & Careers > **Job Hunting**
    #1 in Books > Business & Money > Skills > **Business Writing**

The lesson I learned is to write about what other people want to read enough to purchase a book about the subject. Figure out other people's passions and write about those things.

It can be extremely frustrating to write a book that doesn't sell. Sometimes, no matter what you do, nobody wants to buy it. It's important not to take this personally. There is always a good reason a book is not selling.

Maybe the cover is not attractive enough, the book description doesn't entice your customers, or the "look inside" only contains copyright information and not a sample of the writing. Your book could be in the wrong category, have poorly chosen keywords, or be competing with other books that are much higher in the rankings.

One reason a book won't sell is that the subject is not popular. It won't sell if no one is interested.

Indeed, a book on different ways to peel potatoes might interest you, but you may have trouble finding people who want to pay money to read what you've written. There are some subjects that are so unpopular that people won't even accept free downloads for their Kindles.

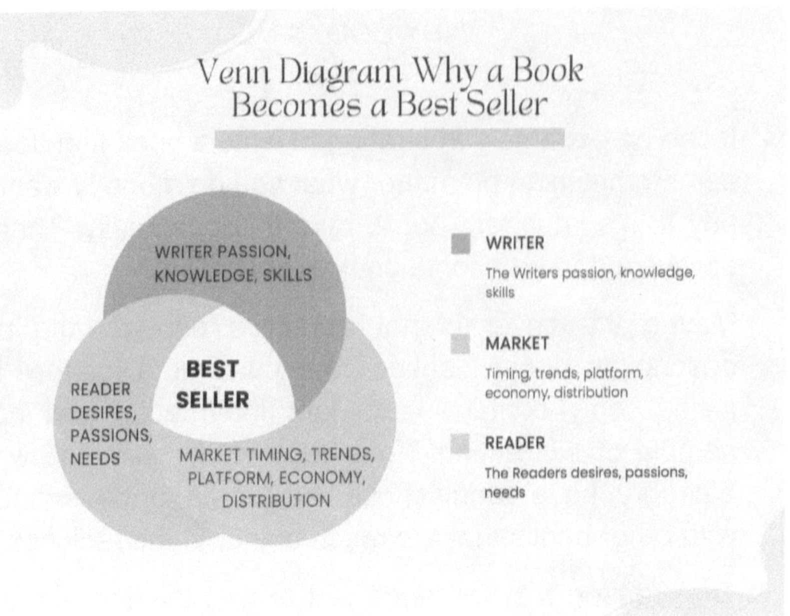

The Venn diagram above reveals why some books become bestsellers while others languish in obscurity. Your book might have everything going for it–interesting content, professional editing, and an attractive cover–yet still cannot find its audience. The missing piece often lies in understanding that bestselling books don't just happen by accident.

A book needs three critical elements working together. First, you must bring something valuable to the table–your unique knowledge, hard-earned skills, and genuine passion for the subject. Without this foundation, your book lacks authenticity and depth. Second, there must be readers who want what you're offering. They need to have genuine desires, passions, and needs that align with your content. A brilliantly written book about an obscure topic that interests only a handful of people will struggle to find commercial success.

But here's what many authors miss: even when your expertise perfectly matches reader demand, market conditions can make or break your book's success. The timing might be wrong, the platform algorithms might not favor your category, economic conditions could affect spending on books, or distribution channels might not be benefiting you. A book only becomes a bestseller where all three circles intersect–where your knowledge and skills meet genuine reader demand within a market that's ready for it.

Exercise–Get a piece of paper and spend a few minutes writing down a list of your passions, experiences, knowledge and skills. Don't overcomplicate this exercise– keep it quick and to the point.

For example, my list is:

Passions: Human Rights; Writing; Photography

Skills: Computer security; management, leadership; writing; photography

Knowledge: American history; the Roman Empire

Experiences: Bullied in school; Trip across the southwest; Hiking in Joshua Tree; Being manager and leader; Going on a cruise; Being married; Caring for chronically ill person for 8 years

Take the time to make this kind of list for yourself. Don't worry about whether these topics will sell–we'll get to that later.

MINING YOUR LIFE FOR NONFICTION BOOK IDEAS

Beyond your major life experiences and developed skills, there's a goldmine of book ideas hiding in your everyday routines and observations. The key is learning to see the ordinary through fresh eyes.

Consider your work environment. I've held jobs ranging from retail clerk to corporate executive, and each workplace taught me something that others struggle with. When I worked in a liquor store, I learned how to stay calm under extreme pressure while coordinating multiple tasks simultaneously. That's a skill millions of people desperately need to develop.

Your hobbies and interests, no matter how niche they seem, represent potential audiences. I collect fantasy miniatures, which might sound obscure, but there's an entire community of enthusiasts who would value a guide on painting techniques. Even something as simple as your approach to organizing your home office could become a productivity book.

Pay attention to the questions people ask you repeatedly. Friends and colleagues often seek your advice on specific topics, which signals that you have knowledge others want. For years, people asked me how I read so many books while working full time. That recurring question could become the foundation for a time management guide.

Your struggles and failures offer rich material. The business I started taught me about entrepreneurship. The eight years I spent living with a chronically ill led to insights into the medical profession that would give a personal look at the healthcare system.

Family dynamics provide endless inspiration. The way you handled caring for aging parents, navigating divorce, or raising difficult teenagers could guide others facing similar challenges. Even positive family traditions–like annual camping trips that teach children self-reliance–can become the basis for parenting or family lifestyle books.

Look at your community involvement too. Volunteering at the local animal shelter, serving on the school board, or organizing neighborhood events all develop expertise that others need. Fundraising strategies for supporting your local church or enhancing your community library could easily fill a book for other volunteer organizations.

The problems you solve daily without thinking about are book ideas in disguise.

How do you manage a tight budget?

How do you maintain friendships over long distances?

How do you stay motivated during extensive projects?

These everyday solutions, when systematized and explained, become valuable guides for others facing the same challenges.

MINING YOUR LIFE FOR FICTION STORIES

Fiction draws from the same well as nonfiction–your experiences, observations, and imagination–but transforms them into stories that explore deeper truths about human nature.

The people you've encountered throughout your life provide endless character inspiration. That eccentric neighbor who collected lawn gnomes and talked to them each morning, could become the protagonist of a quirky literary novel. The ruthless boss who made my early career miserable became the foundation for a corporate thriller villain. Even brief encounters matter—the homeless veteran I met at a bus stop, who told me three sentences about his time in Afghanistan, can form the foundation of an entire war story.

Family secrets and tensions offer rich material for fiction. Every family has mysteries, conflicts, and unspoken truths that can fuel dramatic narratives. The great-aunt who supposedly ran away to join the circus in 1952, but whom family members whisper about in contradictory ways, could anchor a multi-generational saga. A bitter divorce, viewed through a child's eyes and reimagined with different outcomes, can be written as a coming-of-age novel.

Your own emotional experiences, when filtered through fictional characters, allow you to explore feelings safely. The anxiety I felt during my first job interview transformed into a psychological thriller about corporate espionage. The loneliness of moving to a new city became a romance novel about finding connection in unexpected places.

Historical events you've witnessed or studied closely provide authentic backdrops for stories. I lived through the dot-com boom and crash, giving me firsthand knowledge of that era's optimism and devastation—the perfect setting for a novel about ambition and failure. My fascination with World War II, combined with research into resistance movements, could become the basis of a spy thriller set in occupied France.

"What if" scenarios from your own life generate interesting plots.

What if I had taken that job offer in Tokyo instead of staying home?

What if my high school girlfriend and I had gotten married?

What if my father hadn't died when I was twenty?

These alternate possibilities, explored through fictional characters, create emotionally resonant stories.

Workplace dynamics translate beautifully into fiction. The office politics at my corporate job, the camaraderie among restaurant staff during busy shifts, the tensions in academic departments—all these environments contain natural drama, conflict, and character relationships that readers recognize and connect with.

Even your fears and nightmares provide story material. The recurring dream about being trapped in an elevator could expand into a claustrophobic horror story. Anxiety about identity theft can evolve into a paranoid thriller about digital surveillance.

Local settings you know intimately give your fiction authenticity that readers can sense. The small mountain town where I grew up, with its gossip networks and hidden scandals, might become the setting for a mystery series. The urban neighborhood I lived in during graduate school, with its mix of gentrification and longtime residents, may provide the backdrop for a literary novel about changing communities.

- What experiences have influenced and touched you deeply?

- What do you know about well?
- What skills are you adept at?
- Who have you known and loved?
- What hobbies bring you joy?

Exercise–Make a list of potential topics without worrying about whether anybody else is interested in them. You can prune that list down later, but the first thing is to understand that you've learned awesome things, you have unique abilities, you've gone through trials and tribulations, and you've known kick-ass people. These things are potential book topics.

Finding an Interesting Topic

One of the great things about being a self-published author is that you can write about anything you want. Whatever wild idea comes into your head is fair game, assuming it's not illegal or obscene [5], as a subject for a book. This freedom to write and publish anything is unprecedented in history, and you should certainly take advantage of the opportunity to make your thoughts, feelings, and knowledge known to others.

Unfortunately, writing and publishing a book, and making money from it are two entirely different things.

There are several points in creating your book that are critical for earning a profit as a writer. The first, and

---

[5] Obscenity violates the terms and conditions of most publishing platforms.

arguably the most important point, becomes relevant before you have even begun work on the book.

If you just write about things willy-nilly and publish a book about any random plot that's of interest to you, then more than likely your books will not sell well.

That's why it is of utmost importance that you learn how to research the book's marketplace before you put a single word down into your manuscript. Even a little bit of research can prevent you from spinning your wheels on topics that don't sell any books and help you to positively focus on ones that can make you some reward.

For example, I'm a computer security expert, and used my skills at Trader Joe's for over twenty years. As I mentioned earlier, the first book that I wrote without doing any market research, was about how to secure your home computer. I was convinced that this would sell well because, in my mind, "who wouldn't want to have a secure computer?"

Much to my surprise, it turns out that people simply are not interested in spending the time or money to lock down their computer systems. All they want to do is buy a product, install it, and forget about it, or they depend on the manufacturer to worry about security.

The book's profits didn't even cover its own costs. I wasn't discouraged, because by that time I had already published and written several more books, some of which were selling and making money.

Later, I performed some basic research on moneymaking topics and found that many people were interested in making money while working from home. Because of that, I began writing a series of books on how to do exactly that.

Having learned the right lessons, these sold relatively well without heavy promotion.

There are vast numbers of ways that you can do research about topics for your fiction or nonfiction books.

LIBRARIES

How long has it been since you visited your local library? If you don't already know, find out where your local library is located, and head on over. You'll be pleasantly surprised at what you'll find. The people who work in your library live and breathe books, and you'll discover that by talking to them, you can get a good feel for subjects and topics that are popular amongst readers. While you're there, see if there are any writing or other related groups that meet occasionally. Then, make it a point to visit them.

Exercise–Visit your local library and discuss possible topics with the librarians. Don't forget to chat with the volunteer workers (often college students) as they will often have a good idea of what currently interests people. While you are there, get a library card and visit at least once a month. Librarians are great friends to writers, and you will find their knowledge and experience invaluable.

BOOKSTORES

I'm sure there's at least one bookstore in your local area. The people who work in these establishments understand books and know what is selling. They are constantly exposed to the book-buying public–exactly the type of people you are looking for and need to understand.

Exercise–Visit two local bookstores: a large chain bookstore and a smaller, mom-and-pop establishment. Take a few hours, scan the shelves; see what's selling, talk to the people who work there, and even to some patrons. Also, take the time to find out if there are any local groups that meet or at least advertise in the bookstore. Make a point of introducing yourself to the manager and assistant manager–they can become great resources as you establish yourself as a local writer.

MEETUPS

If you want to find people who are interested in similar topics, head over to a site that is now ubiquitous and synonymous to the idea: Meetup.com. Join and search for meetups on topics that are of interest. These can be hit or miss, but I found meetup groups are quite a good way to meet people, get into some conversations, and find out what books they're interested in buying. You can almost certainly find several meetup groups within driving distance, about topics of interest to you.

Exercise–Join www.meetup.com if you haven't already and use their search function to find local writing groups. There is probably one or even more within driving distance. Visit those groups, find one or two whose vibe you like, and become a regular member.

Also, look for groups that match your interests. If you enjoy sewing and knitting, and that's what you want to write about, then find some local groups that do those activities, join them, and become a regular member.

Amazon is the largest "bookstore" in the world, and it will become your primary market when you publish your books. It's important that you understand the tools available to help you as an author.

Go to the Amazon search bar and enter a keyword or phrase describing your book. Search for books with that keyword. For example, if your book is about selling on eBay, enter *selling on eBay* into the search bar.

Click on the first book, assuming it is about the correct subject, and scroll to the Product Details section.

A sample is shown below.

Product Details

Series: Earn Money from Your Home
Paperback: 132 pages
Publisher: The Writing King (August 4, 2016)
Language: English
ISBN-10: 1943517363
ISBN-13: 978-1943517367
Product Dimensions: 6 x 0.3 x 9 inches
Shipping Weight: 1.6 ounces (View shipping rates and policies)
Average Customer Review: ★★★★☆ (25 customer reviews)
Amazon Best Sellers Rank: #93,948 in Books (See Top 100 in Books)
#13 in Books > Computers & Technology > Internet & Social Media > **eBay**
#92 in Books > Business & Money > Small Business & Entrepreneurship > **Home Based**

Look at the "Amazon Best Sellers Rank" field. That number reflects how well the book is selling. Search for several books using your keyword or phrase. Once you have about a dozen, try a related keyword such as "make money on eBay" and repeat the search. Then click a category on the first book's page and note how books in that category rank.

In the above example, this is:

Books>Computers & Technology>Internet & Social Media>eBay

Starting with the first book in that category (ignore books that are not related to your topic) repeat the same procedure as above to get the number of sales per week for a dozen books.

You can repeat this procedure with other categories to get a good idea of how well your topic is selling.

Once you've searched half a dozen terms and checked a few categories, look at the pattern. Are books on that topic selling 1 copy per week? 20 copies? Hundreds of copies?

If the books you find are selling thousands or tens of thousands of copies, then the keyword or phrase is very competitive. It is difficult to get your book noticed because the better selling books will always be listed ahead of yours.

If you consistently see values of 0 or 1 for dozens of books, that tells you that this topic is a slow seller.

The ideal is to find a topic that sells good numbers (a thousand copies a week) at the top end but drops off to a few dozen a week or less. If all your findings are in the thousands, that topic is probably way too competitive for you to do well.

This is a very simple, albeit time-consuming, exercise, and many people have come up with other methods.

KDSpy (kdspy.com) is a browser extension that speeds up manual Amazon research. Install it, browse Amazon, and KDSpy pulls sales-rank, price, estimated sales, reviews, and a simple color indicator for Popularity, Potential, and Competition. Green lights suggest the niche has workable demand. Yellow or red means the niche will be harder to break into. Use KDSpy to scan categories and keywords quickly, but treat its sales and revenue numbers as estimates rather than exact figures because they are calculated from rank data and public Amazon information.

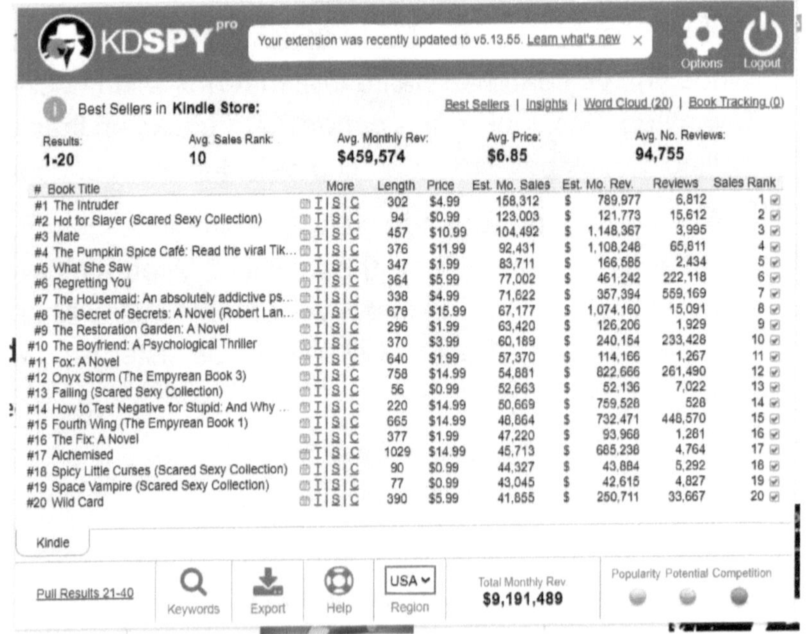

Results:	Avg. Sales Rank:	Avg. Monthly Rev:	Avg. Price:	Avg. No. Reviews:
1-20	10	$459,574	$6.85	94,755

# Book Title	More	Length	Price	Est. Mo. Sales	Est. Mo. Rev.	Reviews	Sales Rank
#1 The Intruder	I | S | C	302	$4.99	158,312	$ 789,977	6,812	1
#2 Hot for Slayer (Scared Sexy Collection)	I | S | C	94	$0.99	123,003	$ 121,773	15,612	2
#3 Mate	I | S | C	457	$10.99	104,492	$ 1,148,367	3,995	3
#4 The Pumpkin Spice Café: Read the viral Tik...	I | S | C	376	$11.99	92,431	$ 1,108,248	65,811	4
#5 What She Saw	I | S | C	347	$1.99	83,711	$ 166,585	2,434	5
#6 Regretting You	I | S | C	364	$5.99	77,002	$ 461,242	222,118	6
#7 The Housemaid: An absolutely addictive ps...	I | S | C	338	$4.99	71,622	$ 357,394	559,169	7
#8 The Secret of Secrets: A Novel (Robert Lan...	I | S | C	678	$15.99	67,177	$ 1,074,160	15,091	8
#9 The Restoration Garden: A Novel	I | S | C	296	$1.99	63,420	$ 126,206	1,929	9
#10 The Boyfriend: A Psychological Thriller	I | S | C	370	$3.99	60,189	$ 240,154	233,428	10
#11 Fox: A Novel	I | S | C	640	$1.99	57,370	$ 114,166	1,267	11
#12 Onyx Storm (The Empyrean Book 3)	I | S | C	758	$14.99	54,881	$ 822,666	261,490	12
#13 Falling (Scared Sexy Collection)	I | S | C	56	$0.99	52,663	$ 52,136	7,022	13
#14 How to Test Negative for Stupid: And Why ...	I | S | C	220	$14.99	50,669	$ 759,528	528	14
#15 Fourth Wing (The Empyrean Book 1)	I | S | C	665	$14.99	48,864	$ 732,471	448,570	15
#16 The Fix: A Novel	I | S | C	377	$1.99	47,220	$ 93,968	1,281	16
#17 Alchemised	I | S | C	1029	$14.99	45,713	$ 685,238	4,764	17
#18 Spicy Little Curses (Scared Sexy Collection)	I | S | C	90	$0.99	44,327	$ 43,884	5,292	18
#19 Space Vampire (Scared Sexy Collection)	I | S | C	77	$0.99	43,045	$ 42,615	4,827	19
#20 Wild Card	I | S | C	390	$5.99	41,855	$ 250,711	33,667	20

Exercise–Spend some time examining the sales statistics of books within your topic/category to find out if they're selling. Search for your subject and select a few books, one at a time. On each book page, look at the Product Details section and find the "Amazon Best Sellers Rank". Follow the procedure described at the beginning of this section to familiarize yourself with book rankings.

FACEBOOK AND OTHER SOCIAL MEDIA

As an author, you should be very active on social media outlets such as Facebook, BookTok, Pinterest, Instagram, LinkedIn, and Goodreads at least. Join groups that pertain to your topics and spend some time getting into online conversations with people in those groups about their interests and likelihood of purchasing books on certain subjects. You'll learn what is selling and what isn't from these conversations. Keep in mind that your purpose is only to do research and avoid the temptation to sell your own books.

Exercise–Get into a few conversations on social media about book topics and subjects of interest to you as an author. Search for groups about your topics, join, and take part in conversations. Over the long term, do this regularly (several times a week) to build a fan base of interested readers.

ARTIFICIAL INTELLIGENCE

AI offers a powerful way to uncover interesting writing topics. These tools analyze vast amounts of online data, including trending news, popular search queries, and social media discussions. By processing this information,

AI identifies patterns, emerging interests, and gaps in existing content.

For example, AI can spot rising trends across various niches by examining search engine data and news. This helps pinpoint topics gaining traction. AI-powered tools also generate extensive keyword lists related to a broad subject, showing search volume and competition. This allows you to find specific, high-demand angles within a larger topic.

AI can perform content gap analysis, comparing existing articles to identify areas where information is scarce or could be expanded. This helps you create unique and valuable content. By analyzing discussions on forums and social media, AI also reveals what questions people are asking and what problems they need solved, providing direct insight into audience needs. This makes AI an effective assistant for discovering viable writing subjects.

One topic research decision worth thinking about early: series versus standalone. An author and writing coach I interviewed made a deliberate commercial decision to write in series. Her reasoning: if Book One goes well, it is much easier to sell Book Two to the same audience than to sell a completely new concept to a new audience. The readers who liked Book One already trust you. Her five-year plan is to have three substantial series running simultaneously. That's a catalog strategy built into the research and planning stage, before a word is written.

Do your research before you write. Check Amazon, walk into bookstores, talk to readers. None of it is foolproof, but even basic market research can save you months of work on a book nobody wants to buy.

This matters even more when you're publishing a lot of books. Speed without targeting is just faster failure. The authors who build sustainable catalogs aren't the ones who write the most — they're the ones who write the most books in topics people are actually looking for. Research is what separates a productive catalog from a pile of books nobody finds.

Chapter 3: Writing

If you're going to be a self-published author, you must write books. Well, that's not totally true in all cases. It is possible to hire ghostwriters to do the work of writing, but that's outside of the scope of this manuscript. [6] Our focus here is only on writers who self-publish their own works.

To be an author, you must write. It doesn't matter what gets in the way–writer's block, malicious people with critical comments, grammar Nazis, family, friends, emergencies, and everything else–you must find time to write.

I block out about 50% of my work time every day to spend writing. The other 50% is split between other tasks such as promotion, publishing, networking, and so forth. The

____

[6] See my book *The Ghostwriting Advantage* for more information about how ghostwriting works.

reason for this is that I'm a writer, and the primary characteristic of a writer is writing.

Exercise–For one or more days, keep a notebook with you and note down everything you do. Be sure to include work, play, travel (including commuting), time with the kids and family, TV watching, video game playing, goofing around, and everything else. Don't make any evaluations about anything–just note what you did, and the time spent.

Once you've got a list (three days is best to catch a wide spectrum and cross-section of activities) examine it and determine which activities are required and which are optional. With that information, could you create enough time during the day to write? You'll need at least 4 hours a day. Work out what you can do to increase your writing time.

CHOOSE YOUR WRITING TOOLS

How will you do your writing? Do you prefer handwriting, using a typewriter, typing into a computer, or speaking the words into your word processor? Maybe you prefer talking to a recording device and transcribing that into digital form. According to an interview, *50 Shades of Grey* was written on a Blackberry, and I'm sure many books have been written on iPads, smartphones, or other devices.

Whatever tool you choose for writing, make sure that it works well for you. Using the incorrect tools, poor applications, slow computers, and so forth will slow you down, leave you frustrated, and might lead to writer's block.

If you want a dedicated writing application, Scrivener is worth a look. It stores research, chapters, and scenes in a single project, lets you reorder material with a corkboard and outliner, and compiles to .docx, ePub, and Kindle-ready files.

Hardware doesn't need to be expensive. For travel, I use a cheap tablet under $300 that runs web apps and dictation software well enough to get drafts done. Fast and stable matters more than flashy.

The advantage of using dictation software is that most people talk several times faster than they can type. For example, I can type between 1,500 and 2,000 words per hour, but I can dictate over 2,000 to 4,000 words per hour. Of course, in both cases, I need to read through what I've written to edit out any mistakes.

As a writer, your word processor, computer (or smartphone, iPad, or even Blackberry) and email system are your most important physical tools. If they are slow or crash often, you will lose productivity, which means your writing will be slower and you will be frustrated and unhappy.

Choose a word processor and computing resources that are fast, don't crash, and help, rather than hinder your writing.

If you enjoy very rudimentary approaches, like a typewriter or pen and paper, simply make sure it is the most efficient and enjoyable way for you to write.

Make sure your word processor has an excellent built-in grammar and spell-checker. You shouldn't depend on these totally, but they can help reduce the number of errors that pop up in your writing. This is important if you use dictation software, because the automatic grammar and spell-checker can fix many dictation errors.

If you can't afford a good word processor, you can use Microsoft Office 365 online or Google docs. Office 365 online is far superior in functionality compared to Google Docs, but both are free and do an excellent job.

A major advantage of using the online versions (either Google Docs or Office 365) is that your documents are stored in the cloud and not on your computer. Thus, if your system crashes, your documents will be unaffected. You can edit them from any computer that can access the web.

Exercise–Spend some time checking out both Office 365 online and Google Docs. If you don't have one already, create an account on each, and compare them by functionality and speed. You might avoid spending any money by using one of these applications, assuming they are fast enough to keep up with your writing.

Your Writing Routine

One problem that writers have is that they sit in a chair for many hours at a time, typing on a keyboard or talking into a microphone. This can lead to obesity, health problems, backaches, knee pain, headaches, and a host of other issues. It can also make a writer irritable and argumentative.

To ease these problems, write for a certain amount of time, say 45 minutes, and then get up and do something physically active for 15 minutes.

I set a timer on my desk for 45 minutes and write for that amount of time. When the timer dings, I get up and take a walk, make lunch, go out on the deck and stare into space, or do anything else other than write.

My chiropractor recommended doing this to help with back pain. It works like a charm, and I find it interesting that working for several hours in a row is less productive than taking a 15-minute break every 45 minutes.

Exercise–In the morning, write for three hours without taking a break. Take a break for lunch, and then in the afternoon, write for 45 minutes and take a 15-minute break three times in a row.

Afterwards, take note of the differences in how you felt about your productivity while practicing each of these two methods.

An author and coach I interviewed framed this simply: schedule your writing time and follow it. When that time comes, be committed to putting something on the page. Don't overthink it or overanalyze — just write from the heart. The message is what matters. You can go back and correct everything later. Getting it down is the job.

A writer I interviewed had a useful framing for this: accept that writing is both an art and a craft. You can learn the craft. What's harder to learn is the art. He's accepted that he's more craftsman than artist, and that's what can be most directly improved. His advice: sit down, write lots, write rubbish. Then realize it's rubbish, work out how to improve it, and write better. That cycle is the whole process.

Your Voice and Style

The most important thing you need to do once you decide to become a self-published author is to find your voice and style. This is true for any kind of artist, whether they are painters, sculptors, writers, pottery makers, weavers, and even actors and actresses.

You can be taught the mechanics of writing, but only experience will guide you to the creation of your own point of view, style, and voice. Once you break out of the mundane sameness you were taught in formalized courses, your writing career will really take off.

Besides, you'll feel a lot more satisfied writing books from your heart. You'll find that once you master using your own viewpoint and style, writing becomes a joy and you'll look forward to the times that you spend transforming your thoughts into book form.

How do you bring out these qualities in your writing?

It starts with one simple statement:

Write.

You must write consistently and constantly for several hours every day.

Exercise–Everyone is passionate about something in their life. Write a one-page essay that is related to your passion. Don't worry about spelling, grammar, or style. Just write it.

Next, write a page about something you understand but doesn't generate any passion in your heart.

Compare the two. Notice any differences in the way they read? Which one is better? Which did you enjoy writing more?

WRITING EVERY DAY

To be a writer, you must write. That might seem to be an easy decision, but it needs to be said and repeated because quite a few people say they are writers or authors but have trouble sitting down and getting their words into a manuscript, whether it be digital, typed, or handwritten.

There are many other things too needed to get your works ready for publication, including finding an audience, marketing to that audience, publishing your books, and so forth, but the long and short of it is—this is worth repeating ad infinitum—that to be a writer you must write.

The best way to learn to write is to do it often and to get critique from your peers about what you've written. If you're going to be a professional in this field, work your way up to writing at least a thousand words at a minimum every single day.

I know, I know. I can hear you voicing your objections. Some of you are telling yourselves that I'm crazy or don't understand the situation. You might say you don't have time to write that much because of work and family life. You could tell me you feel fortunate if you can get a couple of hundred words written.

You could even say that a goal of, say, two thousand words a day, or even a week, is unrealistic, especially for you in your circumstances. How can anyone write that much and still take care of their other responsibilities?

An interesting fact of life is that people put energy into what's important to them. Conversely, if an activity is unimportant, then people will not put in the requisite time and energy to be successful in that area.

This presents an easy way to tell the importance of something to someone: they will put in the time, effort, and energy into that activity. You can use this information to separate what is real or factual from what they are just saying.

If you believe that your writing is important, for whatever reason, then devote the time, energy and effort necessary to become a professional.

Writing is not an easy occupation and trying to make a living as a self-published author is even more difficult, if only because you also need to learn and master so many other specialties.

Before you commit to becoming a writer in the genuine sense of the word, ask yourself if you're willing to put in the time and effort to make it happen.

I'll reiterate; to succeed, the primary thing that you need to do, day in and day out, every single day of the week, is write as many words as you can.

Exercise–Write a one-page essay or story in an area where you feel impassioned. If you love (or think you'll love) mystery writing, then write a quick mystery. Once you are finished, describe how you feel.

The best example of writing discipline I've encountered came from an interview with a bestselling author who has published well over a hundred novels. She has written when sick. Written when her mother died. Written while in the depths of depression — which for her is an ongoing condition, not an occasional one. Written when the power was out, the house was freezing, and the only electricity came from a generator. The only time she did not write was when her cruise ship was caught in a severe storm — a former North Sea military vessel in near-crisis conditions, passengers on alert for a possible abandon-ship order. The laptop would have been flying off her lap. That was her excuse. One time. Everything else, she wrote.

Her rule: set an absolute minimum word count and meet it every day, no matter what. Not a goal. Not a target. An absolute. That's what separates the authors who finish books from the ones who are always working on one.

A novelist I interviewed put it directly: consider writing a long game, a marathon not a sprint. First step is to write the damn book. So many people talk about writing, she said, without ever completing one. Her own approach when in writing mode is a chapter a day. Her books average around 36 chapters, so a first draft takes about six weeks. She then spends far more time editing than writing. The writing is the fast part. The shaping is the work.

A self-published novelist I interviewed writes on trains, planes — anywhere she can. When she gets stuck on one part, she skips it and starts a bit later in the book, then comes back. Her tool for capturing ideas on the go is Evernote: if she has five minutes waiting somewhere, she types something and pastes it into the manuscript later. Every scrap of writing time counts.

SET A DAILY QUOTA

I found that the best way to ensure that I write enough each day is to set a goal or quota in the morning for how many words I'm going to complete by the time the day is over.

When I get up, I look at my calendar and see what is scheduled–I also do ghostwriting, blogging, and other services for clients–and set a quota based upon how many hours are left in the day. I make it a point to write at least four hours each day, and complete at least 1,000 words an hour (by completion I mean dictated and reviewed twice).

A good rule is to allocate at least 50% of the workable time in a day towards writing self-published books. Publishing, promoting, and all the other tasks, including those needed for paying clients, take up the other 50%.

My standard word quota for each day is 5,000 words for the books that I am authoring. I can write 10,000 words in a single day, every day of the week, but I find that it's best to ensure that what I write is ready for the proofreader by the time the day is finished. That way I don't have to confront a very large number of words that need to be edited and proofread all at once.

Exercise–In the morning, when you get up, set a quota for how much you will write that day. Meet that quota. Was it overwhelming, or a walk in the park? Find a challenging pace and adjust as needed.

SHOW, DON'T TELL

A fiction author I interviewed described his approach to scene-building this way: before you write, imagine the world you're entering. What does it look like? What does it feel like? Then connect it to something you've actually experienced. He used the example of San Francisco at night when the city releases flow-throughs beneath the streets — standing near one of those openings, the smell is described as death. He takes that sensory memory, asks himself how it made him feel, and puts that feeling into the scene.

People don't want to be told a story. They want to follow along, feel the character's emotions, and find a way to connect. The difference between a reader who finishes your book and one who puts it down after three chapters is almost always this: did the scene make them feel something? Craft the feeling first. The details that support it will follow.

WRITE THEN EDIT

One of the best ways to slow down your pace and introduce writer's block is to edit at the same time as you write. When you write, simply write. Don't keep going back to re-edit the same line or paragraph over and over.

Many authors don't understand that the purpose of the first draft is simply to get their thoughts down into their manuscripts in some semblance of order. There is no need for it to be publishable, polished, or even readable.

You know how it goes: write a sentence, review that sentence, rewrite a word or two, review it again, rewrite a few more words, review again, delete the whole thing, write it again, and, after a while you may then find yourself stuck and unable to write.

Don't do that. Instead, type or dictate the words as quickly as you can and don't look back–until later.

The concept is to get your ideas and words out of your head and onto the page or digital paper. Editing while you are writing slows down the process to a crawl. If you do it too much, writer's block will rear its ugly head, and you'll find yourself unable to proceed.

Once you've written a certain amount of text, go back and make a pass to edit it and make it more readable. My practice is to write an entire chapter, using voice dictation, and then go back and edit that chapter separately.

You'll find that keeping these two tasks separate makes authoring a book much quicker because writing requires a different set of skills than editing.

Exercise–Write a one-page essay about any subject and edit it as you go along. When you are finished with that, write another page without editing, then go back and edit it afterwards. Did you notice any difference?

The same novelist described it as carving wood: get the basic form first, then whittle it down. Writing is the creative part of the brain. Editing is the critical part. They don't work well at the same time, and trying to use both simultaneously is what kills momentum and produces writer's block. Get the shape on the page. Then polish it.

It's quite common for an author to keep a writer's journal with them everywhere they go. This is usually a notebook and is often handwritten, but many use a tablet or their smartphone.

In a writing journal, you can jot down notes, phrases, ideas, concepts, or thoughts wherever you are.

I've never been attracted to the idea of a writing journal because my mind doesn't work that way. My style is to sit down in front of a computer for blocks of time–a whole morning, afternoon, or evening–and keep writing until I've met my minimum word count or time goal for the day at the very least. If I feel very motivated, then I continue writing past my goal. However, regardless of how I feel, the goal must be met.

Some authors keep meticulous notes throughout the day of anything that pops into their heads. I've known several who fill up huge notebooks with their inspirations, various and rambling thoughts.

Keep notes of ideas for stories, books or articles. If you don't do this, you'll kick yourself when you can't quite remember the brilliant idea that came to you in the middle of the night or while walking in the park.

A writing journal can be an outstanding tool, and it can help you build your writing skills. Just remember, you probably won't be using the words in your journals for your books, promotional materials, and other publishable works, so it should not be counted as part of your quota for the day.

Exercise–Use your notebook for a week. Write your thoughts, ideas, and so forth whenever you can, and at the end of the week look over what you have done. Is a writing journal something that helps you or is it unnecessary?

LEARNING TO WRITE

You're probably wondering at this point when I'm going to share the secret of how to learn to actually write.

On a formal and obvious level, there are many opportunities to learn the craft of writing. Classes are always available at your local colleges, universities, and trade schools, as well as the obvious online sources, as webinars and tutorials, which can have the advantage of being more personalized.

Some of these classes and courses have a good value; they educate you on the mechanics you'll need, such as grammar, spelling, structure, formatting, and so forth. They may also go into other subjects such as how to promote your work, find an audience, or beef up your social media.

The typical college course on creative writing can teach you a few things about how to write, but channels creativity into specific, "safe" and normal areas and formats.

For example, if you take a college course about writing mystery stories, you're going to learn how to write a standard, soup to nuts mystery, including the basics of plot, structure, characters, and so forth. There is value in learning in this manner.

By the end of that class, you will be able to write the exact same type of mystery story that everyone else publishes.

The problem with that is that it churns out predictable, mass market stories, which is great if your sights are aimed at the safe and average, but not so good if you want to sell a lot of self-published books or become a bestselling mystery author.

To achieve those higher goals, your writing must stand out and outshine the competition. The best way to do that is to inject yourself–your unique viewpoint, style, and so forth– into your writing.

You should be constantly learning and taking as many courses as you can afford. Visit Udemy.com for an excellent selection of short, highly focused classes that don't cost an arm and a leg.

I've also found that junior colleges are an inexpensive and accessible method to get the basics that you'll need to succeed.

There are many online courses that can help, but be careful because, as I've mentioned before, there are quite a few scams in the wild world of the web. Check reviews, instructor credentials, and refund policies before you buy.

If you're seeking academic rigor and formal credentials, Coursera and edX are sound choices, as they partner with top universities to offer accredited courses and even degrees. If your focus is on creative skills and hands-on projects, Skillshare provides a community-driven environment.

For those aiming to boost their tech expertise, Udacity, Pluralsight, and Codecademy offer specialized programs and interactive learning experiences. Meanwhile, MasterClass provides unique insights from world-renowned experts, though it's more for inspiration than practical skill-building.

Udemy Courses

Udemy offers tens of thousands of short courses, often less than an hour long, on focused subjects. You'll find just about everything you want here. Udemy frequently runs specials with course prices as low as $10, so be sure to get on their mailing list to take advantage of their specials.

Avoid spending $9,997, $99 or $19,999.99 for the slick-sounding training that you learned about after sitting through a 2-hour webinar. Use a fraction of that money to purchase exactly what you need from Udemy, your local community college, free online courses from universities and colleges, or focused, low-cost training, pinpointed to specific subjects.

Exercise–Visit Udemy and read through the descriptions of the courses. Sign up for one or two courses (don't overdo it) and take them.

Writing Critique Groups

Once you've learned the basics of writing, perhaps by taking a few courses at your local junior college or online, your best bet for honing your writing skills is to join and attend as many writing critique groups as you can. These are informal get-togethers that occur on a weekly, biweekly or monthly basis where writers read one or two chapters from their works and then the other writers in the group provide critique.

It is important to understand that critique is not criticism. Per the dictionary (Merriam-Webster.com), criticism is:

> *to express disapproval of (someone or something): to talk about the problems or faults of (someone or something)*

> *to look at and make judgments about (something, such as a piece of writing or a work of art)*

Critique is:

> *a careful judgment in which you give your opinion about the good and bad parts of something (such as a piece of writing or a work of art)*

Malicious people gain pleasure from criticizing art and writing. Critical remarks are not helpful and are often intended to cause harm. Your best bet is to ignore them and move on with your life.

Critique is used to improve the quality of your writing. To be useful, critique must be specific and practical. This is one of the primary differences between critique and criticism. Criticism is general without specifics and provides no 'maps' to betterment.

Critique vs Criticism

Understanding critique and criticism effectively

Critique	Criticism
Positive Aimed at fostering improvement and growth.	**Negative** Dismissive feedback
Constructive feedback Provides actionable suggestions for future work.	**Undermining** Emphasizes mistakes rather than solutions or growth.
Encouraging Focused on potential	**Critiquing flaws** Focused on fault-finding
Supportive Often leads to feelings of inadequacy and discouragement.	**Detrimental** Can harm relationships and hinder creativity and progress.

References

Insights from psychology and communication studies

The purpose of writing groups is to give and receive useful and practical feedback on various aspects of your writing.

Some critique groups focus on grammar and punctuation; others are more interested in plot points, characterization and technology. Visit several groups as a guest until you find one or two that you're comfortable with, and then attend as often as possible.

To find groups, join and use Meetup.com. In most areas, you'll find several groups if you search for "writing groups" or "writing critique groups." I found that groups that meet weekly or every other week work best. Monthly meetings just aren't often enough to give enough guidance.

These critique groups can be extremely useful in helping you mold your books–or other forms of writing–into a finished, readable work.

For example, I ran a weekly critique group that specializes in science-fiction stories. The feedback that I received is that a character seemed to change personality from chapter to chapter. It made the book uneven and difficult to read. This was good critique, and by using that input, I rewrote a few paragraphs and made the character much more believable.

My recommendation is to attend as many critique groups as you can fit into your schedule. One or two times a week is a good minimum, and the advice you gain will help you bring out your unique qualities and improve your writing.

Exercise–Join Meetup.com if you are not already a member and search for writing critique groups in your area. If you find one or some that inspires you, make the time to attend, and bring along a few pages from one of your works. Do a reading, listen to the critique from others, and when others read, give them great critique as well.

DICTATING

People often speak faster than they can write, so it makes sense that dictating their words using a feature such as Microsoft Word Dictate or Google Voice will speed things up.

Voice recognition used to be very primitive and problematic, but the kinks have been worked out of this technology, and it now works exceptionally well.

If you use Google Docs, the tool is called Voice typing under the Tools menu. There are two major ways to dictate: speak directly into your document so the words appear in real time or record first and transcribe later.

Microsoft Word includes a "Dictate" option that lets you dictate into a microphone or transcribe a file. I've found its transcription feature to be very good.

For transcription, you can hire services on Fiverr or use Rev and similar sites.

All these methods are perfectly acceptable, and the one you use depends on your own preferences.

Regardless of whether you dictate your words into your manuscript, or whether you write it out using a keyboard, you'll need to make an editing pass or two after you are done.

I like to write, or in my case dictate, a full chapter, then go back and edit that chapter. This eases the barrier of having an entire book to edit all at once when I'm done. How much you write before you edit is up to you, but the minimum amount is probably a chapter.

PROOFREADING

Once I've completed the writing, reviewing and proofreading for the day, I'll go back and read the entire work I did that day, from beginning to end, out loud.

By the time the day is finished, I have several chapters or sections in excellent condition.

Once the entire book has been completed, I do one final proofreading pass from beginning to end. This pass is also done out loud, because in my experience that is the best way to catch errors.

Even after all this editing and proofreading, grammar and spelling errors will still squeak by. Get someone else to look over your manuscript for errors for the final polish.

Check out Fiverr.com for very low-cost proofreaders. Better still, you can exchange services with other writers that you know (you proofread each other's works). This is one advantage of building your writing network.

Of course, you always have the option to hire a professional editor.

Use automated tools to speed checks and catch common errors. Grammarly, ProWritingAid, and AutoCrit each have strengths. Grammarly is quick and easy to use for nonfiction. ProWritingAid gives deeper reports and style analysis. AutoCrit targets fiction and helps spot pacing, repetition, and genre-specific issues.

Also, use the spelling and grammar tools built into your word processor. Microsoft Word 365's Editor has improved substantially compared with older versions, though some advanced checks require an online connection or subscription. No matter the tools you use, plan time for human proofreading and one last read aloud.

Exercise–Write a one-page essay on any subject. Read it out loud and correct any errors. Now go to Fiverr.com and find a proofreader. Submit your manuscript (it will probably cost $5 to $100 depending upon the length). Once it comes back, usually in a few days, examine the results and note how many corrections were made.

USING GENERAL AI TOOLS FOR PROOFREADING

Use general-purpose LLMs like ChatGPT or Claude for idea work, quick rewrites, or phrasing options, not as your final proofread. They hallucinate, miss many mechanical and consistency issues, and can invent problems that do not exist.

Relying on them alone risks introducing factual errors, changing names or dates, mangling punctuation, and missing style inconsistencies.

Instead, use targeted editing tools for proofreading tasks. For grammar and spelling, use tools such as Grammarly, ProWritingAid, or LanguageTool. [7] For style and readability, consider Hemingway or ProWritingAid. For

---

[7] Caution: proofreading tools often find errors that are not errors, especially regarding commas. ProWritingAid and Grammarly love commas and seem to want to insert them everywhere. Use your own judgement instead of taking their suggestions blindly.

reference and citation checks, manual verification against primary sources or dedicated citation tools is best.

A suggested workflow involves drafting and revising with your normal process, then using targeted tools to catch grammar, punctuation, passive voice, and style issues. Next, use a consistency tool or your style sheet to check names, hyphenation, capitalization, and formatting. If you want phrasing alternatives or a quick clarity pass, run a short, narrowly focused prompt through an LLM, but fact-check any changes it suggests against primary sources. Always include a last pass by a human proofreader or trusted beta reader before publication.

INVALIDATIONS AND CRITICISM

We've touched on this before, but it's important, so bear repeating.

Something you must be careful about throughout your writing career, but especially during educational times, is the people who invalidate or criticize your writing.

Writers and artists frequently get attacked by insecure and malicious people in society–these are haters mostly. This is especially true on the Internet, on sites such as YouTube and Facebook, but it can happen anywhere.

When I was in high school, my English teacher read one of my short stories and told me I'd never be a writer. He said my work was boring, mundane, predictable, and difficult to understand. Those comments were exceptionally discouraging since I trusted him as an authority, and this contributed to my failure to move into professional writing until much later in life.

An evaluation can be as subtle as a shrug and a frown after reading a chapter, a biting, sarcastic remark, or a lackluster comment such as "it was okay". These minor criticisms can have quite an impact on an author or artist. Primarily, this is because of the general nature of the comments–there's nothing that can be done, barring a complete rewrite, to rectify the supposed flaws that were implied.

The best strategy is to ignore this type of criticism.

Often, these comments are not meant to be malicious. Perhaps someone is having a bad day, has a headache, or simply hasn't had their coffee yet. Don't antagonize them; just ignore their comments.

Critical remarks can come from anyone: family, friends, or foes. Heck, it can even come from an inexpert source or one whose support and admiration has never been lacking. One never knows what deeper reasons may provoke these negative slurs.

I've found that temporary writer's block often directly results from negativity. Subtle remarks can be the most damaging because they are not always noticed at the time they are said. Instead, these words get buried in the mind, and surface later as barriers or insecurities. This invalidating effect can be magnified because the comments are often strategic or sly and, on some level, meant to cut down.

Be especially wary when reading comments on social media. People can get quite vicious when commenting about books or other creative endeavors, and the remarks can be extremely upsetting and discouraging.

For some odd reason, this is especially true of the comments left on YouTube videos. I've found it's a good idea to avoid reading these comments. Turn off the commenting if you can. I've found through experience that there is very little to gain by leaving your YouTube posts open to comments.

Never reply to negative and unconstructive comments. Never contact the commenter to argue, try to get them to change their mind, or even to solicit more information or feedback. It is not worth the trouble. Contacting these commenters often opens a proverbial can-of-worms, leading to mindless and upsetting threads and discussions.

When someone leaves a negative comment on one of my works, I delete it as soon as possible—if that is an option. There is no value in leaving negativity attached to your work, on your blog, or on your social media.

This only applies when you have control over those postings on YouTube or other social media. You can't delete negative comments on Amazon.com and other sites.

However, read both positive and negative reviews on Amazon and Goodreads. As with anything on the Internet, you will run into occasional harsh criticism for various reasons, but sometimes you'll find a nugget of wisdom. Occasionally, a reader will leave a long, useful review.

Reviews, good and bad, can help you in various ways. You may decide to revise the current book, which is very easy in the self-publishing world, or you can take the comments to heart for your next book.

Ignore criticism and invite critique. Be sure you understand the difference—critique is positive, reinforcing, specific, and practical, while criticism is general, presented negatively, and disheartening.

Exercise—Write an essay of a page about any subject. Ask several people to read it and notice their comments and reactions, then notice your reaction to their comments.

The same bestselling author had two pieces of advice on this that I think about often. First: don't treat your book as your baby. Once it leaves your hands and goes to an editor — or in self-publishing, once it's published — it's no longer yours in the same way. Somebody else is going to do whatever they're going to do with it. Readers will interpret it differently than you intended. Critics will miss the point. That's the deal. Don't think about it. Move on to the next book.

Second: don't read your reviews. They will either make you depressed, angry, or give you an inflated sense of yourself. None of those outcomes helps you write the next book. The people worth listening to are editors and trusted readers who give you specific, actionable feedback. A three-star review from a stranger on Amazon is not feedback. It's noise. Treat it accordingly.

PLAGIARISM

> *I sent a nice email, and he chewed me out, saying he loved my article and was only trying to get it out to people who needed the information. I sent him a letter from my lawyer telling him to take it down, which he did immediately.*

Anything you or anyone else writes is copyrighted from the moment it is created. You do not need to file any special documents or do anything else–the copyright is automatic. [8]

That matters because creative work has value, and if anyone could take it and claim it as their own, creators could not make a living. U.S. copyright law allows fair use, which can permit short quotes or clips for purposes such as review, commentary, or scholarship. Fair use is judged on a case-by-case basis, so brief quotations are common but not guaranteed safe without context.

Outside fair use, copying another work without permission is copyright infringement. Plagiarism is a related but separate issue. Plagiarism is an ethical breach. If you borrow ideas or wording, cite your sources in a standard format such as Chicago or MLA to show your research and maintain credibility. [9]

Copyright infringement is usually a civil matter that can lead to a lawsuit and damages. In rare, willful commercial

---

[8] This is true for the United States. For other countries, check out the copyright laws that apply.

[9] APA (American Psychological Association), the style you probably used in college, is not the appropriate style for books intended for the general public.

cases, criminal charges are possible, but that is uncommon. Registration with the U.S. Copyright Office is optional for ownership, but it has real benefits. Registering online gives you the right to sue in federal court and can make you eligible for statutory damages and attorney fees if you register promptly, usually within three months of publication.

To register a work in the U.S., go to the Copyright Office website, create an account, complete the online form for in the appropriate category, upload a copy of your work, and pay the filing fee. Processing times and fees vary, so plan accordingly. You'll also need to mail a copy of the printed manuscript, if any, to the Library of Congress.

Also, consider how you want others to use your work. If you want to allow reuse under set conditions, use a licensing option such as Creative Commons. Licenses like CC BY or CC BY-SA let you permit sharing while retaining attribution rules and other limits.

Use plagiarism checkers and proofreading tools to catch accidental copying and sloppy attribution. PlagScan is one option. Other tools exist and vary in cost and features. Test a few services to find one that fits your workflow. A final human review is still essential.

> *I will write every day. Most weekdays, I write for about ten hours a day. That doesn't mean eight hours of surfing the net or watching videos on YouTube. I park my butt on a chair and write– I learned that writer's block is a myth created by people who don't have, or understand, a writing process. –*
> **Jonathan Maberry**

Every writer occasionally suffers from what is commonly known as "writer's block," which is a lack of motivation to write. It's disconcerting to be moving along at a good clip, writing thousands of words, and suddenly feel you've run head-on into a wall.

Sometimes squeezing out a single word is painful and writing an entire paragraph can take hours, or even a whole day. Occasionally, writer's block can be so severe that writing ceases for days, weeks, months, or even years at a time.

What causes this?

Many things.

Long stretches of staring at a computer screen can drain motivation and focus. I've found that no matter how driven I am, hours upon hours at a keyboard eventually slow my output to a crawl.

Negative remarks are another common cause. A frown, a sarcastic line, or a lukewarm "it was okay" can burrow into your confidence and resurface later as doubt or stalled work. For writers who pour their hearts into words, that invalidation can be especially damaging.

Practical causes matter too. Poor sleep, poor diet, alcohol, recreational drugs, and some prescription medications can blunt creativity and concentration.

Highly charged life events such as divorce, the death of a loved one, conflict at work, or exposure to abuse and toxicity will also sap your ability to write. In those cases, your emotional energy is correctly occupied elsewhere.

I handle screen fatigue with a strict schedule. I set a timer for forty-five minutes, write hard, then stop when the buzzer goes off and spend fifteen minutes away from the computer. The break must be away from screens. A short walk, an errand, a quick visit with a neighbor, or just standing outside clears the eyes and resets the mind.

When personal turmoil is the issue, I journal the feelings or talk it through with a close friend. Turning raw emotion into private notes keeps it from blocking creative work. If the block coincides with persistent low mood, anxiety, or worsening function, seek help from a therapist or your doctor. [10]

Negativity from others is a separate problem. Ignore outright malice, invite specific critique, and do not engage with trolls. Subtle comments can be the worst because they offer no clear fix. If you have control over a platform, delete toxic posts and close comment sections that add no value. When you cannot remove criticism, read reviews for practical points and use what helps.

---

[10] Professional treatment, including therapy and medication when appropriate, can address underlying depression or anxiety that interfere with writing. Do not change or stop prescribed medication without consulting a clinician.

Sometimes, writer's block comes down to discipline and routine. Separate drafting from editing. Write first, edit later. Keep a habit that gets words written even on bad days. For many writers, a sensible rule is to finish a chapter before deep editing, or to set a daily word target. Recognize the block for what it often is: temporary and often traceable to routine, life issues, or health.

If your goal is to make a living as a self-published author, treat writing like a job. You cannot afford to let extended spells of inactivity become the norm. Understand the problem, apply reasonable fixes, and keep moving forward.

THE GRAMMAR NAZIS

An author I interviewed whose day job is disaster relief was in the US Virgin Islands after a major hurricane when his computer died after seven years of use. Getting a replacement shipped there was nearly impossible. He typed on his phone for about a month and a half. He just kept going. That's the standard. Whatever the obstacle — environment, equipment, circumstance — you find a way and keep writing.

The same author was blunt on this: she doesn't believe in the muse, or inspiration, or writer's block. You sit down, apply yourself, and write. That's the whole process. Waiting for the right feeling or the right moment is how people spend years talking about a book they never finish.

In your writing career, you will run into the "Grammar Nazi," a slang term for the person who obsessively enforces grammar, punctuation, and usage rules. They spot typos, correct comma choices, and call out split infinitives and sentence fragments.

This is defined as:

> *A person who habitually corrects or criticizes the language usage of others.–Wiktionary.com*

Some of these people provide useful copyediting that improves clarity. Many are pedants who value form over meaning and can shut down a writer with tone or timing. Learn from consistent, specific corrections, and ignore petty nitpicking. In critique groups, state upfront whether you want line edits or big-picture feedback and stick to that boundary.

A Grammar Nazi will flag a sentence like, "The writer quickly ran to the store," insisting it should be "The writer ran quickly to the store" because adverbs should not split infinitives, even though "to run quickly" is perfectly clear. They might also demand that you never begin a sentence with "And" or "But" despite their common use in modern prose for emphasis or flow.

Another favorite target is the Oxford comma, with the complaint that its omission creates ambiguity even when context makes the meaning plain. These are the kinds of minor points that rarely hinder comprehension but often become battlegrounds for pedants. [11]

---

[11] The Oxford comma, also called the serial comma, is the comma placed before the conjunction in a list of three or more items. Example: "apples, oranges, and bananas." The comma after "oranges" is the Oxford comma. Its

Some classes say your book must be free of grammar and spelling errors. That is true in principle, but taken to extremes, it makes your life harder than it needs to be. Your book does not have to be perfect. No matter how many proofreads you do or how many professionals read it, occasional errors will slip through. That is part of being an author.

People I call Grammar Nazis love to hunt those few mistakes. I got a three-star review that said, "This book was good except for the grammar and spelling errors peppered throughout the manuscript." My first negative review had me rereading the entire book three times over several days, and I found one spelling error and two tiny, debatable grammar issues.

Most readers forgive a few slips. When someone emails specific errors with page numbers, I fix them and thank the reader. Do the same. Correct obvious mistakes, but do not let a single review derail you.

Do the best proofreading you can. Read your work aloud, send it to a professional proofreader, and then read it again. For most books, that is enough. Use your time wisely and focus on what gets meaningful results: clarity, structure, and reader experience. Your book must be professional, not flawless.

Aim for a balance between quantity and quality. Finish the book, get it into good shape, publish, and then correct what needs fixing rather than chasing an impossible perfect version.

---

use is a matter of style rather than a strict grammatical rule, and it can prevent ambiguity.

Write every day and publish fast. Quality matters, but a well-researched, proofread book that gets published beats a perfect book that never ships. Get it written, get it out, and move on to the next one.

The writing routine you build here — the daily quota, the dictation habit, the write-then-edit discipline — isn't just about productivity. It's the infrastructure that makes publishing a lot of books possible without burning out. Authors who grind themselves into the ground usually do so because they write in bursts with no system. Get the process right and the volume takes care of itself.

Chapter 4: How to Effectively Use AI in Your Writing Life

Let me be direct about something before we go further. AI will not write your book for you. I've seen what happens when people try — technically correct sentences strung together into something that has the shape of a book but none of the substance. No voice. No genuine insight. No real experience behind the words. Readers can feel the absence even if they can't name it, and they don't come back for the next one.

What AI can do is make you a faster, better-informed, more productive author. Think of it as a digital assistant — one that never sleeps, never gets bored, and can turn around research, copy variations, and structural feedback in seconds. Used that way, it's one of the most useful tools that has ever landed in a self-published author's hands.

Used as a replacement for actual thinking and actual writing, it's a shortcut to mediocrity.

I use Claude as my primary AI tool. For cover imagery I use Leonardo.ai. That's it. There are dozens of other tools out there — some of which I'll mention in this chapter — but my advice is to pick one or two that fit your workflow and learn them well rather than chasing every new release.

WHERE AI ACTUALLY HELPS

Research and topic validation. Before you write a book, you need to know whether anyone wants to read it. AI can dramatically speed up this process. Ask it what questions people are asking about your topic, what gaps exist in the current books on Amazon, what angles haven't been covered. It won't replace the Amazon and bookstore research described in Chapter 2 — remember that AI often fabricates facts and sales data — but it's excellent for generating angles and identifying what you might have missed.

Titles, subtitles, and book descriptions. This is where AI earns its keep for most authors. Give it your book's main idea, your target reader, and the core benefit, and ask for twenty title variations. Most will be unusable. Three or four will be genuinely interesting. The same process works for book descriptions — give it your structure and ask for a hook, an emotional opening paragraph, and a benefits list. You'll rewrite everything, but having raw material to react to is faster than staring at a blank screen.

Cover image prompts. My workflow for book covers uses Claude to craft the image prompt and Leonardo.ai to generate the background image, which I then polish in Paint Shop Pro. Getting a good image prompt is harder than it sounds — you need to specify style, mood, color palette, composition, and what to avoid. Claude is good at turning a vague idea into a detailed, specific prompt that actually produces usable results from image generators.

Marketing copy. Email subject lines, social media posts, ad copy, author bio variations — these are all short-form tasks where AI can generate a dozen options quickly and you pick the one that sounds most like you. Don't publish the AI output directly. Use it as a draft and rewrite in your own voice.

Proofreading assistance. Tools like ProWritingAid and AutoCrit can catch errors and flag patterns — passive voice, repeated words, pacing issues — that you'll miss because you're too close to your own work. The caveat is that these tools generate a lot of data, and a lot of it is noise. False positives are common. Treat the output as a starting point, not a verdict. Look at the flags that repeat across multiple sections. Ignore the ones that contradict your style. And still do your own read-aloud pass — it catches things the tools don't.

Structural feedback for fiction. This is one of the more genuinely useful applications for novelists. Paste in your manuscript or a chapter and ask AI to identify where the pacing sags, where character arcs lose consistency, where scenes are missing emotional beats, and where dialogue could carry more weight. It won't give you the rewrite — that's your job — but it can surface structural problems that a human critique group might take months to identify.

Brainstorming and unsticking. When you're stuck on a chapter, a plot problem, or how to explain a complex idea, AI is a useful thinking partner. Describe the problem and ask for ten different approaches. You probably won't use any of them directly, but one will usually trigger the idea you actually needed.

WHERE AI FAILS

Writing your book. I've seen the output. It\'s crap. Grammatically correct, structurally passable, utterly hollow. No genuine experience behind it, no real voice, no specific details that could only come from someone who actually knows the subject. Amazon is already filling up with AI-generated books and readers are getting good at recognizing them. Don't do it.

Fact-checking. AI lies with confidence. It will invent citations, misstate dates, fabricate statistics, and get biographical details wrong — and it will do all of this in the same authoritative tone it uses when it's completely accurate. Never use AI output as a source. Use it to generate questions, then verify the answers yourself through primary sources.

Replacing your voice. Your voice is why readers buy your next book. It\'s built from your actual experience, your opinions, your specific way of seeing things. The moment you let AI rewrite your prose rather than assist your process, you start sanding that away. Polish with AI if you must. Write with your own hands.

The AI tool landscape changes fast enough that any specific list I give you will be partially outdated by the time you read it. With that caveat, here are the categories and leading tools as of 2026.

General AI assistants. Claude (Anthropic) and ChatGPT (OpenAI) are the two most capable general-purpose tools. Both handle research, brainstorming, copy generation, and structural analysis. I use Claude. There is a meaningful difference worth knowing: Claude is designed with a stronger emphasis on privacy and security than most competitors. It is less likely to use your conversations to train future models, and Anthropic has made responsible AI a core part of how Claude is built. For authors uploading manuscript drafts, ghostwriting material, client content, or proprietary research, that matters. ChatGPT works well too, but if you are handling sensitive material, Claude is the safer choice. The paid versions of either are worth it for serious use — the free tiers have limits that will frustrate you quickly.

Image generation. Leonardo.ai is my tool for cover image backgrounds. Midjourney and Adobe Firefly are strong alternatives. All require prompt skill — the better your prompt, the better your output. Use Claude or another AI to help craft the prompt if you're struggling to get what you want.

Writing and editing assistance. ProWritingAid and AutoCrit both offer detailed manuscript analysis. ProWritingAid is stronger for nonfiction — style, passive voice, readability. AutoCrit is more focused on fiction — pacing, dialogue, genre conventions. Grammarly handles fast grammar and spelling checks. All of them generate more data than you need, so approach them with filters in mind: look for patterns, ignore one-off flags, and trust your own ear over any algorithm.

Audiobook production. AI-generated narration has improved dramatically. ElevenLabs produces realistic voices that can narrate a full book in hours rather than the days or weeks a human narrator requires. The output isn't quite at human narrator quality for nuanced performance, but it\'s good enough for most nonfiction. If you\'re on the fence about producing an audiobook because of the cost and time, AI narration removes that barrier.

Keyword and category research. KDSpy and KDRocket (covered in Chapter 11) do their specific job better than a general AI can. Use them for Amazon-specific research. Use a general AI to brainstorm keyword angles and topic framing before you run them through the dedicated tools.

AI AND THE FUTURE OF WRITING

Here\'s my honest read on where this goes.

AI raises the floor. Anyone can now produce grammatically correct, passable prose. Most of what gets generated without real human input is crap — readable crap, maybe, but crap. The average quality of a self-published book will not improve because of AI. The volume will increase and the signal-to-noise ratio will get worse. But AI doesn't raise the ceiling. It can't produce the kind of writing that comes from lived experience, genuine expertise, and a distinctive point of view. Those things still require a human being who has actually done something worth writing about.

The authors who will struggle are the ones who were already producing generic, undifferentiated content — because AI can now do that faster and cheaper than they can. The authors who will be fine are the ones with something real to say, a genuine voice, and the discipline to keep publishing. That\'s been the formula for success in self-publishing since the beginning. AI doesn\'t change it. It just makes the contrast sharper.

Ghostwriting and book coaching will not be replaced. Clients don\'t hire ghostwriters because they can\'t produce words — they hire them because they can\'t produce their words, organized into a book that represents them well. AI makes the ghostwriter\'s research and drafting faster, but the judgment, the interviewing, the shaping of someone else\'s story — that\'s human work and will remain so.

The ethical line is simple. Use AI to work better. Don\'t use it to deceive readers about what they\'re getting. Disclose AI involvement when it\'s material — particularly for AI-generated imagery on covers, AI-narrated audiobooks, and any significant AI contribution to the text itself. The publishing industry is still working out its standards on this, but readers deserve to know what they\'re buying. Getting ahead of that expectation is good practice and good business.

Conclusions

Use AI as the digital assistant it is. Let it speed up your research, sharpen your copy, generate your cover prompts, and flag structural problems in your manuscript. Don\'t let it write your book. The authors with real experience and genuine voice have nothing to fear from AI — and a lot of useful tools to pick up.

Chapter 5: Building Your Brand

As your writing career proceeds, it is important to focus on building your brand. A brand is the image that you (or your persona under a pen name) portray to other people.

Your brand is closely related to your author platform, which is the method used to portray that image. The two are usually discussed as separate specialties, but there is a lot of overlap between the subjects.

One of the most critical components of your brand and your platform is your author blog. Because it's so important, Chapter 6 is entirely devoted to the subject.

Inevitably, you encounter countless brands throughout the day as you watch television, listen to the radio, surf the Internet, read books and magazines, and go about your daily life. A soft drink company might create a brand based on being refreshing and invigorating, while a businessman leading an ethics-based company could want his brand to portray him as a philanthropist involved in high-profile social projects and charities.

Your brand (or brands) is important because it allows readers to know, like and trust you. The more readers trust you, regardless of whether it's nonfiction or fiction, the more they like you, and the more they feel they know who you are, the more likely they are to purchase your books, write positive reviews, and tell their friends about you.

You may have one main brand, perhaps one for you as an author. Or you may have multiple brands, possibly one for each pen name you write under. Keep in mind, though, that each brand you create and develop requires that more effort, which takes away from your daily writing and promotional routine.

You portray your brand in several ways.

- In your author biography in each of your books.
- On your blog via articles, the about page, and photos or drawings.
- What you post on social media.
- During speaking engagements and book signings.
- From interviews on podcasts and radio shows (and if you can swing it, television).

Exercise–Look up four websites of your favorite authors. What brand do they portray? Are they doing a good or bad job of projecting that image?

YOUR SUBJECTS OR GENRES

Probably the first decision you'll make when defining your author's brand is deciding what you're going to write about.

- Are you going to write fiction, nonfiction, or both?
- Are you going to narrowly focus on one subject or write about many subjects?
- Is your style humorous, casual, formal, or something else?

These and other questions will help define your brand. For instance, Louis L'Amour branded himself as a Western author, while Agatha Christie was known as a writer of mysteries. If you are looking for a science-fiction novel, you would not go looking in the Agatha Christie or Louis L'Amour sections of the bookstore.

These two authors defined their brand narrowly, and because of that, readers know exactly what kind of story they are going to get. This makes them very comfortable with the relative writing style, the storylines, the characters, and the settings.

That's one reason these two authors became well known and had many bestsellers–readers know what they are going to get, and they know they are going to like what they read.

You can define your brand as anything you want–you can have a narrow focus like Agatha Christie and Louis L'Amour, or you can have a wide focus such as a nonfiction author. You could portray yourself as a security specialist, an expert on writing, or someone knowledgeable and credible at making lots of money.

Spending the time to define and market your brand will go a long way towards increasing your bottom line over the long term.

Exercise–Sit down, get your paper and pen, and write a list of subjects you understand and enjoy, or a list of topics for fictional stories. Do any of these stand out to you as an area you might want to write several books on?

If you want to write about many topics, use pen names to create multiple brands. You can pick almost any name, but do not use the name or a close misspelling of another living author or public figure. Pen names solve the problem of promoting different works under one identity.

Pen names let you publish work you prefer to keep separate from your public persona. For example, a Western novelist might publish erotica under a pen name.

Do not expect pen names to guarantee privacy. Pen names are not secret: agents, editors, proofreaders, beta readers, printers, and publishers will usually know the real author. Contracts, payment, and tax paperwork generally require your legal name. If you want public anonymity, plan how contracts and payments will be handled, for example through an agent, a publisher escrow arrangement, or a legal entity.

Here are some famous pen names and the real names behind them:

CLASSIC LITERATURE:

- Mark Twain (Samuel Clemens)
- George Orwell (Eric Blair)
- Lewis Carroll (Charles Dodgson)
- George Eliot (Mary Ann Evans)
- Voltaire (François-Marie Arouet)

MYSTERY/CRIME:

- Agatha Christie also wrote as Mary Westmacott
- Ruth Rendell also wrote as Barbara Vine
- John le Carré (David Cornwell)
- Ellery Queen (Frederic Dannay and Manfred Lee)

ROMANCE:

- Nora Roberts also writes as J.D. Robb
- Jayne Ann Krentz also writes as Amanda Quick and Jayne Castle

CONTEMPORARY:

- Stephen King wrote as Richard Bachman
- Anne Rice wrote as A.N. Roquelaure
- J.K. Rowling writes crime novels as Robert Galbraith
- Dean Koontz has used dozens of pen names

The reasons authors choose pen names come down to a few practical situations. You want to publish in a genre or on a topic that doesn't fit your main brand. You want to separate work you'd rather not have publicly associated with your name. You want to start fresh after a string of poor sellers. Or you simply want to keep different audiences from bleeding into each other.

I've used pen names myself for both of those reasons — once for a subject I didn't want attached to The Writing King brand, and once when I wrote in a different genre entirely. It's a clean solution. You maintain separate identities without having to build a second real-life persona from scratch.

You can use a pen name on the cover, title page, and copyright page where allowed, and you can promote under that name. Copyright registration and some rights assignments often require disclosure of the legal author, so check with your publisher or an attorney for specifics.

Avoid names that infringe trademarks or impersonate real people, since that can invite legal trouble and confusion among your audience.

Some authors hire ghostwriters to produce books released under a pen name; these arrangements are legal if properly contracted and documented. Keep clear contracts for scope, payment, credits, and rights.

If a book's topic doesn't fit your main brand, a pen name can differentiate it and, if promoted correctly, may help sales. Each pen name requires its own marketing and administration: separate websites or pages, email lists, social accounts, branding assets, and a plan for royalties and taxes. Full anonymity is difficult to guarantee, so set expectations and document how identity and payments will be handled.

Exercise–Come up with a pen name for a few of the subjects you chose in the last exercise.

I've made it a point to be a very well-educated and well-rounded person. I'm knowledgeable about many subjects, including computers, business, leadership, relationships, even stamps and global warming. This is because I read books constantly, watch documentaries, and attend online and in-person courses regularly.

It's a rare week when I haven't read a book, gone through an online course, reviewed somebody else's book, or watched a documentary. In fact, in most weeks I'll do all of the above.

This gives me the advantage of being able to write about a vast variety of subjects, and this is exactly what I have enjoyed doing, as evidenced in my portfolio. I have written books about business, medicine, computers, the Internet of Things, communications, leadership, interpersonal relationships, human rights, interviews I've conducted with interesting people, and à propos to this book and my brand–writing related subjects. Heck, I've even published coloring books.

This flies directly in the face of the advice of many promotional and writing experts. Their advice is to focus on a single niche and become well known as the expert in that area. That advice may or may not be useful depending on your skill level, interests, education, and knowledge.

Indeed, there is significant value and advantage in being "the expert" on a very narrow subject. This allows you to focus your promotional activities to a well-defined audience. It also makes it easier to build a targeted email list, and your blog will be more focused.

Some authors choose an extremely narrow focus for their niche, even to become so particular as to focus on specific flavors of ice cream, Bible verses, or the history of any one type of doll, such as Barbie.

The disadvantage of a narrow niche is that the taste of readers can change over time, and you may lose your audience because the niche is no longer popular.

For instance, if your niche is a single trending topic or political figure, you could find that your audience completely disappears once the news cycle moves on.

Or if you were an expert at creating Sudoku puzzle books, and you have hundreds of them for sale, you could find your sales dropped as that niche was inundated with new authors trying to make a few quick bucks in a perceived lucrative and profitable area.

Another obvious drawback of this approach is that although one can be creative, each narrow topic can become exhausted even after digging deep.

I've chosen to cast a very wide net on the subjects that I write about. Many authors do this, and as I've already touched upon, it's common to use different pen names or pseudonyms for each subject.

For example, you could write books about cooking under one pen name, then write a book series about military history under another name and finally produce a series of erotic books under yet a third name.

Regardless of whether you focus on one subject or write about many, once you find a niche is profitable, it's a good idea to focus a lot of energy in that area. Even though I write about many subjects, once I discovered that moneymaking books are profitable, I devoted much of my promotional energy towards that niche.

How do you find a niche? Look for areas where your passion and other people's passions intersect. I'm passionate about writing and publishing. And with some research, as described in Chapter 2, I determined others are attempting to make a living in this area but are lacking real-world guidance, and thus they are passionate about the subject as well.

Because those passions intersect, I channeled my natural talents, skills, education, experience, and knowledge into that area, and it's likely others will be interested as well and will purchase my books.

It's much easier to find a niche that is already developed than it is to create a new one. In fact, unless you're very lucky, it's virtually impossible to develop a new niche, especially for a beginning author.

A good exercise is to find yourself an inspiring and private corner somewhere and write out all the various subjects where you have education, skills, interest, or passion.

Once you have that list, head over to Amazon and check out the books in those areas. Look at the books on the first page of a search by that subject and see how well they're selling. You can do this by going to a book page and scrolling down to a section titled "Product Details". In that section, you'll find in bold, "Amazon Best Sellers Rank".

If that number is very high, say over a million, that book is not selling very well. If the value is low, in the order of 5000 to 10,000, the book is making good sales. The higher the number, the worse the book sells, and the lower the number, the better it sells.

Check out a dozen books in that niche, and you'll soon get a feel for how well those books are doing. Perform this exercise for every item on your list until you find a niche that works for you. If nothing on your list is selling well, then you may have to widen your horizons and add a few more subjects until you find one that works.

This method is not foolproof by any means. Following this advice, I determined LinkedIn was a very lucrative niche. Unfortunately, it turned out that people were not interested in spending money to develop their LinkedIn profiles. I could give away thousands of copies, sell thousands of them at ninety-nine cents, but once I raised the price to something reasonable, like $4.99, my sales dried up.

There are other methods you can use to help you reinforce your conclusion that a niche is lucrative before you write a book. You can survey people on Facebook or other social media, or in writing or other groups; you can grab a clipboard and walk around the neighborhood and talk to people; or you can even have conversations with patrons at bookstores to find out what they're interested in.

It's a good idea to spend some upfront time determining if a niche will work before you take the effort to write a book.

Remain flexible and write and publish books quickly. That way, if you find a niche is not making sufficient income, you can move on to a different one without having spent a dramatic amount of effort and wasted lots of time.

Exercise–Pick a category on Amazon and select a book. Look at the book detail page and scroll until you find the book details section. Look at the "Amazon Best Sellers

Rank". How well is it doing? Try this for several books in different categories.

Next, get your notebook and visit your local bookstore. Look at what is on the shelves and have a conversation with one of the store employees. See if you can come to an informed conclusion about what sells well.

QUALITY OR QUANTITY?

The other day I was reading an article that said you should begin prepping your social media to expect your book publication at least four, and preferably eight, months before the launch date.

That strategy is useful for a major book, one that you plan to spend a lot of time writing and promoting. However, for books that you write and publish quickly, in a matter of days, you won't be able to do this.

The concept of a book launch comes from the world of traditional publishing, where it often takes a year or more from when a book is submitted to a publisher until it finally appears on the bookshelves at bookstores.

In my case, I have a few books that are important to my "core" brand. These build my credibility and showcase my knowledge, skills and talents, and tend to be 30,000 or more words long.

My strategy is to write a longer book of this nature every few months, then spend the time doing a formal book launch and more significant promotion. In between those longer works, I quickly and efficiently write and publish shorter, straight-to-the point books.

The truth of the matter is that the more books you have for sale—the more titles you have out there—the more money you're going to make. Of course, there's always the odd exception of a book that shoots to the top of the charts either on its own, or after a big promotion.

Speed is an important corollary. The faster you get those books written, proofread, beta read, edited, published, and promoted, the faster you make money. Conversely, the longer you take between books, the less money you make.

This doesn't imply that you should pump out poor-quality books. The point is you need to simplify your process so that you get your books from idea to publication and promotion quickly.

Why is this true?

The simple fact of the matter is that books remain in Amazon's database (or the database of wherever you published it) available to be purchased, from the moment you publish them for as long as you keep them listed. Thus, each book in your portfolio might get sales every day, every week, and every month for the rest of your life.

If you are doing some basic promotion for each book, Amazon Ads is ideal for this purpose, then you'll potentially continue to make anywhere from a few dollars to a few hundred dollars each month from every book that you have published. Of course, some books will not sell at all during a single month; however, others may sell hundreds of copies.

The key points to remember are:

- Publish as many good books as you can, as fast as your process allows. By now you understand why: each book added to your catalog is a permanent revenue stream, and the catalog itself becomes your credential. When a ghostwriting or coaching prospect looks you up, they don't see someone who wrote a book — they see someone who clearly knows what they're doing.
- Ensure that these books are of high quality.
- Ensure your promotional materials–which include the book cover, description, title, book reviews, and so on–are up to snuff.
- Use Amazon Ads and other promotional methods to drive traffic to your books.

The reason I keep mentioning Amazon Ads is practical: once campaigns are set up and tuned to produce traffic, they can run with minimal daily effort and support a portfolio of titles. That makes paid ads ideal for backing many books at once.

They are not truly set-and-forget, though. Bids, keywords, and creatives drift, so campaigns need periodic review and occasional adjustment.

It's much easier to focus on one book than it is to focus on many. As a result, any way you can automate the process, especially promotion-wise, will be helpful in improving your profits and reducing your efforts.

Think of a book as a product that you're selling to an audience. Your book may sell very well or, what's most likely, you'll sell a few dozen copies, especially if you don't promote it properly.

If you have only one book to sell, regardless of how well it does, you're only going to profit from that one product. It may sell great for a short period (unless you're lucky or have a lot of money to spend on promotion) but eventually sales will sag, and the money will stop coming in.

If you have a large quantity of books, spikes and valleys amongst titles or categories will balance themselves out to help you maintain a steadier flow of income.

How much time should you spend on each book?

Spend as much time as you need to have a book of reasonable quality that delivers your message the way you desire. My production goal is to take an 8,000-to 12,000-word book from idea to published product in three to five days.

At that speed, I can publish one to three books of that size every week. That's if I'm working on writing books steadily with no interruptions such as freelance writing assignments (for pay), vacations, or anything else.

My minimum goal is to publish one book per week. That gives me time for paid freelance writing gigs, promoting specific books, writing products, putting together courses, and other things.

Speed of publication, or the quantity of books you desire to write and publish, is a decision that you'll have to make. A lot of it depends on how much time you have available to write, whether your writing is a career or just a hobby, and the amount of knowledge and experience you possess regarding your niche or subjects.

The colors, styles and fonts that you choose for your blog, promotional materials, advertising, business cards, and everything else say something to your readers.

Purple has meant royalty for millennia, red means danger or energy, while green or brown may suggest the outdoors.

I recently published a book, *Networking Your Business*, and created a red cover. After consulting with a design expert, she told me that red means anger or emotion, which is great for a self-help book. However, for business, a calmer color such as blue would be better for my audience. I took her advice.

The most important characteristic when you pick a font is that it is readable. This is especially true on the cover of a book, where the first view by a reader is of a thumbnail.

Some fonts portray sincerity or romance; some envision child-like fantasy, while others suggest stylishness.

The styles that you use within your blog pages and elsewhere can communicate a lot more than you might think. Blocky images may portray a more structured or practical style, while circular images could suggest more creativity or fluidity.

Even the positioning of images and fonts can make a difference in the appeal of a book cover. A sloppy cover with titles that are not properly centered, fonts that don't line up, and images that are seemingly randomly placed will look amateurish, and that will not lead to better sales.

Professional designers deal with decisions about which fonts, styles and colors to use all the time. Choosing the right combination is an important decision for your brand, and it's best to get the advice of someone who has been trained in the area before committing to anything.

This doesn't mean you shouldn't create your blog, business cards, and do the promotion. My own materials went through several iterations before I finally met with an artistic designer who helped me create the brand that portrays an image that feels exactly right. The Writing King symbolizes the qualities of royalty, such as self-assuredness and influence, so it was important to me that the colors, fonts, and styles generated that mental picture.

Exercise–Surf to several websites and note how the different fonts, colors, and styles work together–or how they don't.

Logo

One of the most important elements of your brand is its logo. Your logo should be simple with only a few colors (and it should look good in black-and-white as well) so it is easily recognized and memorable.

Display your logo on your business cards, website or blog, stationery, invoices, on your book cover pages, and just about everywhere else that may be seen by your customers or readers.

It's important that the logo portrays whatever characteristics are central to your brand in an obvious and meaningful way.

Don't choose a logo from a stock logo or image site and don't use sites such as Fiverr.com for this purpose. Instead, engage the services of a professional logo designer if possible. This is a specialty that requires a certain degree of artistic talent along with specialized training. I was amazed, after trying with four or five different people, at the level of quality I got from a real professional.

For example, I hired a local company, *Laura's Design Studio*, and she created my logo and helped design my website. Meeting with someone in person to design a logo or a website is an entirely different, and much more fulfilling, experience than trying to work with them over the web.

This is my logo.

The value of meeting with someone in person to communicate your requirements, talk about revisions, and build a relationship so that they truly understand what you want is something that cannot easily be done over the web.

The relationship matters. Your designer will ensure you get the correct file types for print and web. Once you have your logo, you can build off it and create your brand.

You can expect to pay a minimum of $200 for a simple logo by a professional graphics designer, and the price can go up to $500 or even $1,000 for more complex designs.

If you can't afford to pay a graphic designer directly, explore the idea of trading services. For example, you could trade writing copy on their website or a few blog articles for a good logo design.

Make sure you get all the source files for the logo, so you're not stuck with working with the same designer.

Your logo files should be delivered in vector graphics so that it can be resized without losing any details. Get a black and white version for promotion that is not printed in color.

Exercise–Look at the logos of several major companies (from their websites) such as LinkedIn, eBay, Coca-Cola, and so on. Note how the logo delivers a message reinforcing corporate branding.

AUTHOR BIO

Many writers overlook or downgrade the importance of an author biography. That's unfortunate, because a good bio section can improve your relationship with your readers, give information to the media, and help improve your brand and reputation.

Remember, you will improve your sales by getting your readers to know, like and trust you; this concept is explained fully in my book *Networking Your Business*. A biography helps to address the "know" portion of this formula.

A well-written bio targeted to the brand that you are trying to portray helps readers make up their minds, not just to buy your book, but to follow you and see what other books, and possibly products you have for sale.

This is especially true when working with the media. If you're going to do public speaking, book signings, or give interviews for podcasts, radio, and television, having an author bio provides information about you in an easily accessible place.

You want to make your bio interesting, engaging, and directed wholly towards your brand. You want to answer the question, "what makes you the expert about this book (or books or book series) you have written?"

Author biographies are often written in the third person, as if someone were telling your readers about you, although first-person can work occasionally.

Your job in writing your bio is to tell readers why you are an authority on the subject of your book. What makes you an authority and why should anyone care about what you have written?

Include information such as:

- Awards that you have won.
- Books you have written.
- Speeches you have given.
- Articles you've published.
- Articles and other materials published about you.
- Podcasts you've appeared on.
- Interviews you've received.
- Any other honors that you have received that reinforce your credibility.
- Exclude anything that has little or nothing to do with your brand.

Don't worry if you don't get it right the first time. Your author biography, especially the one on your blog or website, should be an organic document that changes. After all, you will ideally publish more books, receive more honors and awards, make more speeches, and so forth.

Where does your bio appear?

- On the About page of your website. This should be the longest and most complete version.
- In the back of each of your books.
- In the biography section of Amazon Author Central.
- On your LinkedIn, Facebook, and other social media profiles.
- On your Facebook pages.
- On various association websites.
- In your Meetup.com profile.
- As part of your media kit.
- In the back of each book written. I create an About the Author for each book that is tailored for the subject. Every book has a different one.
- Anywhere else that asks for a biography or profile.

These profiles should not be identical, but they must tell a consistent story about you and your brand. Tailor each version to its audience and format while keeping the core message the same.

How important is the author's biography? Very. A clear, relevant bio convinces readers, booksellers, and librarians that you can deliver the book's promise. Put yourself in a librarian's shoes: with limited budget and shelf space, they want to know whether you are the right person to serve their patrons before they order a title.

Your bio is a central part of your branding and promotion. Get it right, create multiple variations for different uses, and update it regularly as your credentials, projects, and achievements change.

When crafting your author biography for public platforms, avoid including personal data such as your email address, phone number, or physical address. For security and privacy, direct readers and media to a professional contact form on your website or a dedicated press page.

Publicly visible contact information can be used for spam, doxing, targeted scams, identity theft, and even virtual kidnapping schemes where criminals use scraped personal data to make false threats and demand ransom.

For example, in 2014, YA author Kathleen Hale published an essay about a harsh Goodreads reviewer, then investigated the reviewer herself (including buying background data and driving to the address she believed belonged to the reviewer).

Hale later wrote about those actions in her Guardian piece and in an essay collection. The episode sparked intense online backlash: Goodreads moderation and bans, sustained harassment and doxing aimed at Hale, death-threats and doxing of people connected to the dispute, and a major hit to her early career and publicity.

Note: Caution on using AI to write author bios

Avoid relying on AI to auto-generate your author bio because it produces generic-sounding copy, can invent or misstate facts and credentials, and erases the individual voice that sells books. Feeding personal data into AI can expose sensitive details, and models sometimes reproduce copyrighted phrasing or produce wording that misrepresents experience, creating credibility and legal risks.

Use AI only as a drafting tool: generate headlines, short variations, or bullet-point ideas, then edit heavily to restore your voice. Verify every factual claim, remove any personal data you do not want public, add specific anecdotes and tonal choices that signal authenticity, and run a plagiarism check before publishing. This approach preserves your voice and reduces privacy, accuracy, and reputation risks.

Note: Caution on using Author Bios from Resumes or LinkedIn Profiles

An author bio should never be a mere copy-and-paste from a resume or LinkedIn profile. While those documents highlight professional achievements, they are typically written in a formal, third-person tone that lacks the personal touch essential for connecting with readers. A resume focuses on qualifications for a job, and a LinkedIn profile is geared toward professional networking; neither is designed to capture the unique voice, personality, and creative spirit that define an author.

Your author bio is a direct conversation with your potential readers. It should reflect your authentic voice, offering a glimpse into who you are beyond your professional accolades. This is where you can share what truly drives your writing, your passions, and the unique perspective you bring to your work. By infusing your bio with your genuine voice, you build a more personal connection, inviting readers into your world and making them eager to explore your stories.

Exercise–Set aside a few hours to write your author biography for your blog. Put it aside for a day, then review it and make any corrections you need.

AUTHOR VIDEO

Some people love video, and some hate it. Personally, I fall into the latter category as I'm not very fond of videos of myself. However, there are others who thrive on regular video podcasts or YouTube channels–these people are usually extroverts or have learned to work around their introverted tendencies.

However, an author video, which can be like an author bio in video form, can be a very powerful way to express your brand. After all, the video is the author talking about themselves in their own words.

There are different kinds of author videos possible:

- **Explainer video**–Usually animated and explains something in picture and word form. These are easy to put together and don't require the author to be on camera.
- **Interview video**–A videotaped interview of the author, either made specifically for the purpose, or taken from a media source.
- **Marketing video**–These are created specifically to market an author by a professional service.

- **Podcast video**–If so inclined, an author can put out a regular video series and use the most recent one as their author video.

There are undoubtedly many other kinds of videos that you can create to describe yourself as an author to your readers.

If you decide to create an author video, you can hire a professional service, preferably local to you, to design, shoot, and edit it for you. Creating this kind of video can be complicated, and such specialties such as lighting, makeup, and body position can mean the difference between a mediocre and an excellent video.

Alternately, you can make a video yourself using your smartphone, computer webcam or other device, and edit it using video editing software. These types of homemade videos can be powerful since they are of an author speaking directly to their readers in a natural and real way. If you are going to video yourself, using a tripod (for a digital camera) or a selfie-stick (for a phone) to make it easier.

Exercise–Use your smartphone camera or the webcam on your computer to create a quick, 1-to-3-minute video of you talking about your background.

Author Photo or Image

One of the most important components of your branding package is your author photo. Readers want to physically see their favorite authors because it helps them feel a connection with the writer, and if the photo has the right elements, it will inspire likability and trust.

In most cases, your author photo should be an actual photograph, although in the case of coloring and comic books, an avatar (an image of the author) can be used instead. If you're writing under a pseudonym, and you don't wish to be known under that name, you can use a drawing of a fictional author instead of a photo.

Hire a professional photographer. This is one area of your branding where the money is well spent, and a poor photograph will detract immensely from your credibility.

Hiring a professional photographer isn't as expensive as you might think. I used a Groupon from JC Penney's Photography to get a good headshot for $29.00 and a complete set of 75 photos for about $100.

Some of the types of photographs that you should avoid include:

- **Selfies**–Don't use selfies at all, unless you're writing a book about selfies.
- **Personal photos that are cropped**–Cropped photos just look tacky and amateurish.
- **Photos taken by your friend or associate**–Unless your friend is a professional photographer, you're almost certainly going to wind up with a substandard picture.
- **Outdated photos**–Use a recent photo, not something from high school or college. If you're fifty years old, a photograph of you when you were twenty-two is not appropriate.

- **Photos with other people in the picture**–Sometimes this can be appropriate, such as with a book about your genealogy or family history, but otherwise you should be the only person in the photo.

Instead, your photograph should have the following characteristics:

- **Professional headshot**–A professional headshot, perhaps in black-and-white, works very well.
- **Good lighting**–One reason to use a professional photographer is that they will ensure the lighting is appropriate and makes you look good.
- **Lack of distractions in the background**–The photograph should focus on you and not on the beer bottles, messy kitchen, or pool table in the background.
- **Smiling**–People like to see smiles, so it's important to smile in your photo. A sincere, radiant smile gives you an approachable and friendly appearance.
- **Well-groomed and well dressed**–Make sure you look good for your photo, with a nice haircut or styling and good, clean clothes.
- **Match your brand**–If you write Westerns, then you might wear Western attire. Don't take this too far, but a few subtle touches may add to your brand. For example, if you write Star Trek fanfiction, then you might wear a Star Trek pen on your lapel.

Your author photo should appear in your biography, media packet, and on all social media platforms. Ensure your photos match across all your media.

Replace your headshot at least every couple of years, or more often if your appearance changes significantly. Your picture should reflect your current look, not how you looked years ago. An updated photo can also attract positive attention.

Media Packet

A media packet is a page on your blog containing everything needed for someone in the media to use to write stories in their publications about you.

The media includes television, radio, podcasters, bloggers, newspapers, and other channels used to talk to the public. As you become more popular, and send out press releases and so forth, you're going to get requests for information about you, your book series, your books, and so forth, so it's best to have it already prepared so you don't have to do the work over and over.

I found it's best to create a PDF containing everything in one easy place to make it easy to print out. Don't secure this document as you want anyone to be able to copy and paste from your kit as needed.

Include some or all:

- Introduce yourself and your business.

- Describe your mission–what are you trying to do?
- Include a few testimonials.
- Answer any frequently asked questions.
- List your book series and books.
- Describe any supporting statistics–book sales, bestseller status and so forth.
- Of course, include your primary contact information.

Spend the time to make this document practical, descriptive, and interesting to members of the media. Everything should reflect a positive image of you and your brand.

AMAZON BOOK PAGE

For every book that you publish, Amazon creates a page which includes all the information about it. This showcases your book and is designed to entice people to get the information they need to make a purchase.

The book page consists of one page for each version of your book. Thus, you'll have a page for your Kindle version, paperback, hardcover, and audiobook. Each one of these pages can contain subtly or markedly different information. For example, you can have a different description for your paperback than you do for your hardcover version.

- The front and back covers of your book.

- The "look inside" feature allows people to see the first 10% or so of your book before they purchase. It's important to know that this does not appear right away after you publish–it can take as long as three or four weeks.
- The title, subtitle, and book series.
- The date the book was published. This date does not change if you update the contents of your book.
- The description of your book.
- All the reviews of all your versions are merged on all pages. Thus, you'll see Kindle, paperback, and audiobook reviews, for example, merged on the page for each format.
- A small block containing information about your book such as the number of pages, its ranking, the publisher, and its ranking within each category defined for your book.
- The ASIN or ISBN number of your book. If you specify an ISBN number for your Kindle volume, it will not be listed. Instead, the ASIN is always listed for that format.
- You'll also find advertising for other, similar books, including your own if they apply. This advertising[12] is different for every single person on Amazon, and changes depending upon what they viewed, purchased, and have inside of their wish lists.
- You can include a video trailer for your book on that page, and on the Author's page, you can add your blog, so there is always new content on there,

---

[12] These advertisements are purchased from many sources, including Amazon Ads, which is available to self-published authors.

which allows you to add new trailers to promote all your newest books.

It's important to understand that you have control over most of the information on these pages. You specify the title, subtitle, series, description and publishing company, among other things. For more information, see chapter 10, Metadata.

Most of this information can be changed after you publish the book. For Kindle books, virtually everything can be changed at any time. On paperbacks and hardcovers, the title, subtitle, author, ISBN number, publishing company and series cannot be changed once you've published the book. You can change the information on audiobooks, but you'll have to re-record and resubmit the opening and closing segments if you change the title.

All the versions of a book usually link together on the same book page automatically. If, after a couple of days, this doesn't happen, you can use the "contact" field in your KDP dashboard to ask their support group to do it for you. They are always very happy to help and very competent (send them the ASIN or ISBN for the books you want to link together).

Exercise–Examine several book pages on Amazon and get familiar with all the various parts and sections.

THE BOOK PAGE URL

Each book page is given a unique link (URL) which you can use in your advertising, promotions, and anywhere else to reference your book. The link for any version may be used, since all versions work together on the same page.

https://www.amazon.com/
Real-World-Survival-Preparing-
Surviving/dp/1943517037/ref=asap_bc?ie=UTF8

Above is shown a sample raw link to one of my book pages. The number "1943517037" is the ISBN of that book.

When you use that link anywhere else, remove the "/ref" and everything following as it is unnecessary. Thus, the link above becomes:

https://www.amazon.com/
Real-World-Survival-Preparing-
Surviving/dp/1943517037/

If you have an Amazon affiliate account, then in your promotions and on your blog, include "?tag=affiliate" where "affiliate" is your Amazon affiliate identifier. Thus, the link above using my affiliate ID would become:

https://www.amazon.com/
Real-World-Survival-Preparing-
Surviving/dp/1943517037/?tag=thewritingkin-20

Use short-link and universal-link services to manage your book links, track clicks, and guide readers to their preferred stores.

MyBook.to offers simple, memorable short links for individual Amazon product pages, providing basic click statistics. It's ideal for single-target links, especially for print or spoken mentions.

For example, the link for my book *Real World Survival*:

https://www.amazon.com/Real-World-Survival-Tips-Guide-ebook/dp/B011AI5YUG

Becomes:

http://myBook.to/Disaster

Be sure to trim the book link as described in the previous section (The Book Page URL).

Not only is this easier to remember, MyBook.To also collects statistics on the number of times this link is clicked. This can be valuable in determining if your promotion is working.

For broader distribution, **Books2Read** (Draft2Digital's Universal Book Links) creates a single, geo-targeted link that directs readers to their favorite online retailer, whether for ebooks, audiobooks, or print. This service also allows for custom names, affiliate codes, and detailed analytics.

Choose MyBook.to for straightforward Amazon links. Use Books2Read when your book is available across multiple platforms and you need a versatile, trackable link. Always verify your links before sharing them.

Reliability note

Third-party link services can vanish or change unexpectedly if they're bought out or go out of business. This can break your book links, erase your sales data, stop your affiliate earnings, and undo years of marketing effort.

To protect yourself, always keep a main link you control (like one on your own website), regularly save your sales data and affiliate codes, and have simple store links ready as a backup. This way, you can quickly switch if a service disappears.

Author Central

After you publish your first book, go to:

https://authorcentral.amazon.com/

It is a free dashboard where you manage your author profile and the details that appear on your book pages. Fill every field you can: author bio, author photo, book descriptions, editorial reviews, and available multimedia.

Claim every edition so all formats appear under your name. Upload a high-resolution headshot (minimum 300 by 300 pixels, JPG or PNG). You can upload videos and extra photos, but note that since Amazon's 2022 redesign, additional photos, videos, and blog feeds may not display on U.S. Author Pages the same way they do on some international Amazon sites.

Blog RSS feeds were removed from U.S. Author Pages in 2022, so linking your blog will not guarantee posts appear on Amazon.com. Check whether your regional Author Central supports RSS before relying on it. After making changes, check your profile and allow 24 to 48 hours for updates to appear.

Exercise–Proceed to Author Central and create an account. Look over the options.

DRAFT2DIGITAL AUTHOR PAGE

I use Draft2Digital a lot, and not just as a distribution service. The platform does something Amazon can't: it gets your books into Kobo, Apple Books, Barnes & Noble, and dozens of other retailers simultaneously, with a single upload. For readers who don't buy on Amazon — and there are more of them than most authors assume — D2D is how you reach them.

The D2D Author Page lives at books2read.com and is one of the most useful tools in self-publishing that most authors ignore. Set it up by signing into your Draft2Digital account and completing your author profile — bio, headshot, and book descriptions. Once your books are linked, the page acts as a single destination that shows your entire catalog with buy buttons for every major retailer. You share one link and readers land on a page that routes them to wherever they prefer to shop.

The real value is the Books2Read universal book link. Each of your books gets its own short URL that auto-detects where the reader is located and shows them the right store for their country and preferred platform. One link works for a reader in the UK buying from Kobo, another in the US buying from Amazon, and another in Australia buying from Apple Books. Put this link on your business cards, in your email newsletter, in podcast bios, and anywhere else you promote your books. It removes the friction of asking readers to find your book on their own.

D2D also handles formatting. Upload a clean Word document and it converts it to ePub, MOBI, and other formats automatically. The quality is solid for most nonfiction. For books with complex layouts or lots of images, check the output carefully before distributing.

Royalties through D2D are slightly lower than publishing direct to each retailer, because D2D takes a percentage for the service. For most authors the tradeoff is worth it — one upload, one dashboard, and access to every major platform outside Amazon, rather than managing separate accounts on Kobo, Apple, Barnes & Noble, and a dozen others individually.

Note: if your book is enrolled in KDP Select, you cannot distribute it through D2D or any other platform. KDP Select requires Amazon exclusivity for the 90-day enrollment period. It's a choice you'll have to make for each book — the KDP Select benefits (Kindle Unlimited income, promotional tools) versus wide distribution through D2D. Many authors do both by keeping some titles exclusive to Amazon and distributing others wide through D2D.

Exercise—Create a Draft2Digital account at draft2digital.com and set up your author page at books2read.com. Even if you're not ready to distribute through them yet, claim your author page and get familiar with the interface. Generate a Books2Read universal link for one of your existing books and see how it routes readers to different retailers.

AUTHOR CENTRAL OR DRAFT2DIGITAL AUTHOR PAGE?

Should you use Draft2Digital's author page or author central?

Amazon Author Central focuses on the largest book retailer where many readers make purchasing decisions. Complete your Author Central profile with every available detail: professional headshot, comprehensive bio, book descriptions, and editorial reviews. Claim all book editions so readers see your complete catalog under one name. Amazon's algorithms may favor books with complete author profiles, and readers browsing Amazon often check author pages before buying.

Draft2Digital Author Pages solve the multi-retailer problem. When you share links on social media, in newsletters, or at speaking events, you cannot predict where readers prefer to shop. Some use Apple Books, others choose Kobo, Barnes & Noble, or local bookstores. D2D Author Pages let readers select their preferred retailer instead of forcing them toward Amazon.

The platforms handle different marketing scenarios. Author Central works for readers already browsing Amazon's world. D2D Author Pages work better for external promotion where you need retailer flexibility. Share your D2D link at conferences, in podcast interviews, or on business cards without alienating non-Amazon customers.

Amazon's limitations also justify using both tools. Blog RSS feeds no longer appear on U.S. Author Central pages. Additional photos and videos may not display consistently after Amazon's interface changes. You depend entirely on Amazon's design decisions and functionality updates.

D2D Author Pages give you control over presentation and guaranteed cross-retailer compatibility. Update your profile independently of Amazon's policies and interface modifications.

Using both creates comprehensive coverage. Amazon readers get the full Author Central experience within their preferred platform. Readers from other sources get retailer choice through your D2D page. This approach acknowledges that reader discovery and purchasing patterns vary significantly across different market segments.

Regardless, I recommend you always set up a book page on your own website with all the details about each edition of your book. You should also set up an author bio page on your website.

This covers you in case you lose access toDraft2Digital or Amazon for any reason. It's important to always make sure that you have an option if disaster strikes and you lose your Amazon or other accounts.

I'll be straight with you: I don't run Amazon Ads. I've tried them, they work for some authors, and plenty of people build profitable campaigns with them. But my approach is to focus on organic ranking through good metadata, categories, and keywords rather than paid traffic. That means I'm not the right person to give you deep tactical advice on Amazon Ads campaigns.

What I can tell you is the basics. Amazon Ads is a pay-per-click system — you only pay when someone clicks your ad, not just when they see it. You set a daily budget and a maximum bid per click. Your book must be in Kindle format to advertise, though clicks often lead to paperback and hardcover sales on the same page. You can run automatic campaigns where Amazon chooses the keywords, or manual campaigns where you choose them yourself. Most experienced authors run both.

The key metric is ACOS — Advertising Cost of Sale. It tells you what percentage of your revenue you're spending on ads. If you spend in ads to generate 0 in royalties, your ACOS is 20%. Most authors aim to keep ACOS below 50%, though the right target depends on your royalty margins. Start with a small daily budget of to per campaign, let it run for a few weeks, then cut keywords that spend money without generating sales.

For a proper deep-dive on Amazon Ads, Bryan Cohen's free five-day Amazon Ads challenge is widely recommended by self-publishing authors and costs nothing. Mark Dawson's Ads for Authors course is the paid option most people point to. Either will get you further than anything I could summarize here.

Exercise—Create an Amazon Ads account and read through the help documentation. Don't spend any money yet. Explore the campaign structure, look at keyword options for one of your books, and get comfortable with the interface before you commit a budget.

DRAFT2DIGITAL MARKETING OPTIONS

Draft2Digital offers limited advertising options compared to Amazon's comprehensive ad platform. The service focuses primarily on distribution rather than paid promotion but provides several marketing support features that can complement your broader promotional strategy.

Schedule promotional pricing through your Draft2Digital dashboard for books distributed to participating retailers. Set temporary price reductions or free promotions with specific start and end dates, though not all retailers support promotional pricing and implementation timing varies by platform.

Apple Books, Kobo, and Barnes & Noble typically honor scheduled promotions, while other retailers may require manual price changes. Check each retailer's promotional policies before scheduling since some platforms limit free promotion duration or require advance notice for significant price changes. Monitor your sales dashboard during promotions to track performance across different retailers.

Connect your mailing list service to Draft2Digital's author tools for simplified reader communication. The platform supports integration with major email services including Kit and Mailchimp (not recommended).

Use this feature to capture reader emails through your Author Pages and Book Tabs, then set up automated welcome sequences for new subscribers who discover you through Draft2Digital's tools. Include links to your complete catalog and information about upcoming releases in these sequences.

Submit books for consideration in retailer promotional programs through Draft2Digital's interface. Kobo, Apple Books, and other partners occasionally feature independently published titles in their marketing campaigns, though requirements vary by retailer and promotion type.

Complete all metadata fields and ensure professional cover design and editing before submitting for promotional consideration. Retailers typically feature books with strong sales history and positive reviews, so build your track record before expecting promotional placement.

Connect your social media accounts to your Author Pages for cross-platform promotion and share Universal Book Links across all social channels to drive traffic regardless of follower preferences for different retailers.

The platform generates basic social media graphics for book promotions, though customization options remain limited compared to dedicated design tools. Use these assets for consistent branding across promotional campaigns while supplementing them with more sophisticated graphics created elsewhere.

Draft2Digital's marketing features supplement rather than replace comprehensive book marketing strategies. The platform works best when combined with external advertising, social media marketing, and direct reader engagement efforts rather than serving as your primary promotional tool.

One author I interviewed made a point that stuck with me: people buy into the author as much as the book. Her first YouTube video was filmed in her pajamas. She said, on camera, "This is me. I'm a writer, I work from home, this is what I wear every day." It was authentic, it was real, and it connected. She now has fans in other states — people who weren't her friends before she published, who found her through her content and her honesty about who she actually is.

Being professional and being yourself are not opposites. Show your face. Let people see behind the scenes occasionally. Be consistent — the same person in your emails, your blog posts, your videos, and your books. That consistency is what builds the kind of trust that turns a reader into someone who buys every book you publish.

CONCLUSIONS

Your brand is what helps set you apart from other authors and gives your readers a sense of who you are and why you are credible. Make sure you spend the time and money to build the appropriate image for your niche and personality.

Consistency is the key to creating a good, strong brand that attracts readers and causes them to want to purchase your books. They need to know you (via the author biography and media packet), like you (regular communications) and trust you (deliver quality books).

Most importantly—if you don't take the time to create an author brand, your readers and others will create one for you, without your directed guidance or input. Is that what you really want?

Chapter 6: Author Platform

Your author platform is the stage on which you present your books and your brand to your public. Creating and maintaining a platform is vital to making your books sell and to gaining the interest of booksellers, libraries, and traditional publishers.

How you reach your public depends upon your personality, skills, likes and dislikes. Some authors prefer video, others create audio podcast channels, and others simply blog several times a week.

Regardless of the platform or media you choose, it needs to succeed at attracting and engaging readers. A platform requires a lot of effort, and it's wasted time if it doesn't help build your credibility, increase your sales, and improve engagement.

Think about stretching your boundaries a bit. If you're introverted, try getting interviewed for podcasts or give a speech at your local library. You might be surprised to find that you enjoy those activities.

Regardless of whatever platform you choose, host the materials on your own blog. This gives you a home base for people to find everything about you and your books.

EMAIL LIST

We'll get into Email Lists more thoroughly in Chapter 7.

One of the first tasks on your to-do list is to create and grow an email list. This is your primary way to stay in contact with readers. Use it to send occasional updates about works in progress, new releases, and anything your readers will value.

Start by choosing an email provider. Kit is a common starter option because it offers a free tier and simple automations. Note that free tiers have limits, and pricing can rise as your list grows. Pick a provider that matches your budget and the features you need.

Set up automations. These are emails sent on a schedule after someone signs up. Typical sequence: a welcome message immediately, your bio a few days later, a list of your books after that, then evergreen content or a product pitch. You can add as many messages as you want but keep them evergreen [13], so they do not date themselves.

You can also send one-off campaigns for new books, promotions, and events.

Grow your list by offering a lead magnet, such as a downloadable PDF, a short story, or an exclusive video, in exchange for your reader's name and email address.

Set up your email list when you set up your blog. The blog and list should work together as your main ways to reach readers. An email list plus a blog are essential parts of an author platform.

Include basic legal and deliverability hygiene. Always provide a clear unsubscribe link, follow opt-in rules for your target markets, and authenticate your sending domain if the provider allows it to protect deliverability.

---

[13] Evergreen content remains relevant and useful over time without becoming outdated. Unlike news or trend-based content that loses value quickly, evergreen material continues attracting readers months or years after publication.

An email list is your highest-value direct channel. The single metric to watch is signups. Track list growth, open rates, and conversion to sales.

Exercise–Create an account at Kit.com and go through their help files and tutorials to get an idea of how it works. Does this help you understand how this can help your promotions?

SUBSTACK AND GHOST

Substack and Ghost combine newsletter distribution with website functionality, eliminating the need for separate email marketing services and content management systems. Both platforms handle technical infrastructure while you focus on building readership through consistent content.

Substack operates as an all-in-one publishing platform where you write posts that reach both subscribers and web visitors simultaneously. The platform manages subscriptions, processes payments for paid newsletters, and offers discovery through their publication network. You own your subscriber list and can export it anytime. Substack takes 10% of paid subscriptions but charges nothing for free newsletters. Choose Substack for simplicity and network discovery features, though you sacrifice design control and depend on their feature development.

Ghost functions as a content management system with built-in email capabilities. Use their managed service or install it on your own hosting for complete control over content and design.

Ghost offers sophisticated membership features with free and paid subscription tiers, integrates with payment processors like Stripe, and supports various content formats. Monthly costs vary by subscriber count, but you keep 100% of subscription revenue.

Choose Ghost for more control over presentation, advanced membership features, and custom integrations, though it requires more technical management and higher costs.

Both platforms excel at building direct subscriber relationships that bypass social media algorithms. Regular newsletter content maintains reader connections between book releases and provides ongoing value that strengthens your author brand.

Book Signings

One of the reasons to make your book available in paperback and hardcover is so that you can order copies for yourself to use and sell at book signings.

These events are put on by bookstores, writing associations, local business groups, libraries, and even authors themselves to attract the public and build up buzz about their book. They can last anywhere from thirty minutes to all day and can include one or more authors.

Both the author and the venue have a responsibility to invite people to the signing. Ensure you send invitations to local news sources, your email list, any of your groups, Facebook, and so on. Consider sending out a press release with an announcement to get even more people to attend.

A book tour consisting of multiple book signings in different areas of the city, state, or even country, can do wonders to promote your works. I know from personal experience there's nothing like meeting an author in person, even for just a minute or two, to get their personal note and signature on a copy of their book.

I remember meeting Kelly Reno at the World Mermaid Awards show in Las Vegas in 2011 (I photographed the event). She had a stack of her books on a table and signed a copy of Misadventures & Merfolk, her most recent novel, with a personal message.

Other personally signed books include *Beneath Lies Beauty* by Jacqueline Collen-Tarrolly (a good friend, beautiful model, and actress who played Mauve in the show *Adventures of Sinbad* which ran from 1996 to 1998) and *Showgirl Confidential* by Pleasant Gehman, another great friend and a famous burlesque and belly dancer. Getting signed copies from these authors was a wonderful experience and ensured I'd be on the lookout for their future works.

The point is to create a memorable experience for those who arrive. Be well-dressed, on your best behavior, shake everyone's hand and sell signed copies of your books. Spend the time to talk to everyone and listen, and don't forget to take a few pictures (or even short videos) of you with your fans at these events. These videos and pictures are great for your blog and social media.

You can begin your book signing adventures at your local library. They won't pay you for your time but you will be selling your books to make a few extra dollars.

Your marketing should plan book signings as a regular part of your itinerary for promotion, even if those events are just in your local area. This will help build up buzz in the community about you and your works.

Exercise–Use your favorite search engine to find your local library. Send them an email asking for information about how to set up a book signing.

Jumping into public speaking is one of the most difficult barriers for many authors, yet it is one of the best ways to get your name out there. You can speak at your local Chamber of Commerce, networking meetings, businesses, libraries, special events, conventions, and anywhere else.

To break the ice and learn how to speak in public join a local Toastmasters group. This organization is dedicated to helping people prepare and present speeches, and the cost is low. I'm a member myself, and I recommend that all authors join their local group and attend the meetings regularly.

Record all your speaking events (including those done at Toastmasters meetings) in both audio and video formats, and have someone take pictures. After your speech, send the audio recording to a transcriber. This allows you to use the whole speech, or selected parts, in your promotional materials. [14]

Edit the transcription carefully–it's okay to change it is much as you want–to correct any errors and make it more appropriate for your purposes.

The video and pictures can be used for your book trailers, promotional materials, on your blog, and can even be sent to members of the press. You can also edit videos as desired to use specific portions to suit your needs.

If you do record–either in audio, video or both–your speaking engagements, edit and file them as you go.

---

[14] You may need to get permission from the venue and event host to record.

Otherwise, you'll find yourself with a large backlog of material that is difficult or impossible to search.

Taking the plunge to speak in public about your subject is a wonderful way to improve your credibility and your confidence. You may even find, as I did, much to my surprise, that you enjoy speaking to groups.

Exercise–Visit Toastmasters.Org and find a local Toastmasters near you with a meeting time that you can attend, then visit it as a guest, which is free.

RADIO SHOWS AND PODCASTS

Getting on radio shows and podcasts is a fast way to gain exposure. Use search engines and podcast directories to find shows, send a short email pitch, and offer your expertise as a guest.

Thousands of podcasts exist, and many need guests. If you can speak clearly and answer questions about your book or specialty, you can line up several interviews a week.

To speed up the process, use RadioGuestList and MatchMaker.fm (for best results, each of these options requires a paid subscription). Both services offer paid plans that create a public profile and let you respond to host requests. Highlight your best clips, three topic hooks, and a booking link on your website and YouTube so hosts can vet and book you quickly.

When you agree to appear, clarify recording, editing, and reuse rights up front. Get written permission if you plan to republish the interview. Hosts want a short, specific pitch that includes a one-line bio, suggested topics, availability, and a sample clip or booking link.

Use interviews as content: post show links, short clips, and transcribed excerpts on your website, in your newsletter, and on social channels. Track bookings and follow-ups to avoid duplicate outreach.

Exercise–Visit Radioguestlist.com and get on their email list. Several times a week, you'll receive a list of hosts that need guests. Either email or call these hosts until you get one that agrees to an interview.

SOCIAL MEDIA

Social media is essential for authors who want to build an audience. Use it to engage readers, show your expertise, and start conversations, not just to push sales.

Don't treat every post as an ad. Facebook, Instagram, LinkedIn, Goodreads and other sites reward interaction. Constant, obvious promotion gets ignored. If you only post "buy my book" or "join my Kickstarter," you are not talking to people. You are broadcasting, and broadcasting does not build a relationship.

Post useful, authentic material that reinforces your credibility and invites response. Share short excerpts, behind-the-scenes notes, answers to common questions, guest interviews, photos from events, and links to reviews. Mix value with occasional promotion so readers stay interested and will support you when you ask.

Use platform norms to guide frequency. Some platforms reward frequent posts, others reward fewer, higher-quality posts plus daily engagement. Track what works and lean into it.

Some things you can do that will help include:

- Post questions related to your niche.
- Post links to articles on blogs other than your own.
- Post links to articles on your own blog (note that some groups consider this self-promotion).
- Write short, one or two paragraph articles related to your specialty.
- If visual aids help reinforce your brand or niche, post graphics or images.
- Answer other people's questions, even if they are not related to your niche.
- Treat people with respect, and talk to them as people, not as credit cards or cash machines.

People do not use social media to buy books (with the possible exception of BookTok). They use it to socialize, debate, share, and play. Join the conversation. Educate and entertain. Over time you will gain followers who will buy your books.

Followers buy because they know you, like you, and trust you. Build that with steady, helpful interaction, honest answers, and small doses of personality. When readers know, like, and trust you, they will buy.

Note: Privacy and Safety for Social Media

Keep your personal life separate from your public author presence. Do not post home addresses, real-time schedules, or personal contact details on public pages. Use privacy settings to limit who can see personal posts and photos. Use a PO box or business address and a separate business phone or email for public contact.

Require written permission before sharing photos or recordings of readers. Set clear page and group rules, assign trusted moderators, and use platform tools to remove or block abusive users. If you receive threats or stalking, preserve messages, report to the platform, and contact local law enforcement.

Exercise–Write a couple of paragraphs about a subject that interests readers of your book. Post this on your social media.

FACEBOOK

Alongside YouTube, Facebook remains a key platform for interacting with readers. Create Facebook Pages and Groups for reader interaction. Do not use your personal Facebook profile for reader contact. Ask people to like your Pages and join your Groups instead of sending or accepting friend requests.

Keep your personal life separate from your author presence. If readers are already friends with you, it is not the end of the world but move future audience interactions to Pages and Groups. Check your privacy settings and avoid posting personal schedules, private photos, or other details you do not want broadly visible.

Create a Facebook Page for each significant book or series and one for you as an author. The process is free and straightforward. Use book covers or simple logos as profile images and a clear header image that reinforces the book's message or mood. Use Pages as steady places for news, events, links to reviews, and general updates about your work.

If you do not have a blog, a Facebook Page can serve as a basic public hub. It is not as flexible or controllable as a blog, but it is a free alternative while you build a site.

Post regularly, but not at the cost of quality. Make time each day to engage. Short morning and evening sessions work for many authors: post content, start or join conversations, answer questions, create events, and respond to messages. Create only as many Pages as you can manage well in a 30-minute daily window. Different books draw different audiences, and separate Pages let you keep conversations relevant.

Join groups that match your subject matter. Take part without selling. Contribute useful answers and resources. Over time, members notice you, ask about your work, and may become buyers.

Exercise–Use Facebook's search bar to find writing groups. Join a few of those and introduce yourself. Start taking part in the conversations by asking questions and getting to know people.

Facebook book promotion groups are mostly a waste of time. There are thousands of them. Scroll through any of them and you'll see the same thing: page after page of authors posting covers and blurbs, then leaving. Nobody is reading those posts. The people posting are promoting their own books, not buying anyone else's. It's a write-only channel that looks like a community.

Check the rules before you post anything. Many groups explicitly prohibit promotional posts and will remove you for it. Some Fiverr gigs offer to blast your book to thousands of groups — don't bother. You'll either get banned for violating group rules or post to groups where nobody is listening. Either way you've wasted time and accomplished nothing.

For building reviews and finding real readers, look at BookFunnel and BookSprout. BookFunnel lets you distribute advance reader copies while building your email list. BookSprout connects authors with readers who specifically want to exchange a review for a free copy — a far more targeted approach than posting into empty Facebook groups. Both are worth exploring if your review count is a priority.

LINKEDIN PROFILE

LinkedIn is one of the most important social media platforms for enhancing your brand as an author. Unlike Facebook, LinkedIn is a business social media platform, and everything on it should reflect your professional persona.

If you've already got a LinkedIn profile, go through it with the intent of reworking it to support your brand and your books.

Unlike your author biography, a LinkedIn profile should be written in the first person not the third person. This is because your profile is you telling others about yourself and your specialties.

Everything in the profile should be written to support your niche, your credibility, and the brand that you're trying to build. For example, your educational sections in the profile should include verbiage that describes how your classes and schooling prepared you for your writing career. Each of the positions that you held throughout your life should do the same thing.

The idea is to present a story to those who read your LinkedIn profile which reinforces your credibility and is interesting to those who take the time to read it.

To improve your branding even more, create a company page on LinkedIn to promote your publishing company. You can write a couple of thousand characters about it with some information about your books and so forth.

Your company page can also contain showcase pages. These are very short, each with a paragraph of information about a product or service and a link to a page on your blog. Create one showcase page for each book that you've published, and link to the appropriate descriptive page on Amazon or your blog.

Post an occasional link, short article, video, graphic, or anything else to LinkedIn on a regular schedule. As with Facebook, don't do outright promotion. Your goal is to enlighten your followers to your expertise and knowledge.

Exercise–If you already have a LinkedIn profile, spend some time reviewing it. Does your profile support your career as an author? If you don't have one, then create an account and fill in the blanks in your profile.

GOODREADS

Amazon bought Goodreads in 2013, and the site now funnels readers to Amazon product pages and Kindle options. The interface is clunky, moderation is inconsistent, and review-bombing, harassment, fake listings, and other abuses have become recurring problems.

Use Goodreads only for visibility you cannot get elsewhere. Do not make it your primary platform or your sales hub. Send readers to your own website and email list where you control the message, the links, and the audience.

If you use Goodreads, monitor reviews closely, document any abusive behavior, set alerts for suspicious activity, and be prepared to escalate serious incidents to the platform and to local authorities.

The odd thing about Goodreads is that even though it is owned by Amazon, it is run by a group of volunteers, called librarians, who do everything from helping authors with their books to policing for spammers. There doesn't seem to be anyone truly in charge, which can make it frustrating when you need something out of the ordinary.

As you learn Goodreads, remember it is intended to be a social networking platform for readers. Authors are there to answer questions about their books and interact with people.

Your main purpose on Goodreads is to gain the attention of those who are popular and review books. If you can succeed in getting your book reviewed by a Goodreads influencer in your field, you will probably gain followers and sales. How do you do that? Find the influencers by reading posts and comments. Start commenting and posting yourself in those threads, and once you've started a dialog with an influencer, mention your book.

Unlike Amazon, I've also found that ratings are often left without reviews at all. It can be disconcerting to get 4 or 5 one or two-star ratings without any explanation.

It's just the nature of the beast, and it is best to just ignore the comments, reviews, and ratings entirely. They do not carry over to Amazon unless someone manually enters them in both places.

Consider alternatives and backups for reader discovery and community building so one flawed service does not hold your audience hostage.

Exercise–If you haven't created an account on Goodreads, set one up. Explore the site and start interacting with others.

X

X (formerly Twitter) can work for authors, but use it with limits. Set up an X account that matches your brand, use the same handle in your books, on your website, and in printed materials. Post regularly, include images and clips, and pin a clear profile tweet with links to your author site and mailing list.

Following relevant authors, publishers, reviewers, and readers helps you find an audience. Many will follow back, but follows do not equal engaged readers. Expect short, fast interactions; use threads for longer ideas and media to stop the scroll.

Do not buy followers or use mass-following services. Paid followers are fake or passive, they violate X's terms, and they do not produce sales. Such schemes can also trigger account restrictions. Post everything you create to X, but do not spend endless hours there. Use short daily sessions to post, respond to mentions, and scan lists or inboxes for real conversations.

Exercise–If you don't have an X account, then set one up now. Follow some people you know and read their feeds.

YOUTUBE

YouTube is one of the most important platforms for authors. Create a separate author channel and post videos tied to your brand: author bio clips, explainers, book trailers, readings, interviews, and event footage. Share those videos across your other channels and drive viewers to your website and email list.

BookTok (the book community on TikTok) is highly effective for short, viral clips and discovery, especially for certain genres and younger readers. It is not a straight replacement for YouTube. YouTube is better for long-form content, searchability, and permanent discoverability; BookTok is better for quick viral reach. Use both where they make sense.

Aim for consistency. A weekly video is a strong goal; every other week is acceptable if quality suffers. Your videos do not need to be polished studio productions. Short clips from signings, a five-minute author talk, or edited highlights from events work fine. Capture more than you need and cut it into short clips for reuse.

Vimeo and other hosts are fine for controlled distribution or higher quality embeds, but they lack YouTube's search and reach. Facebook favors native video uploads, so upload a native copy there as well rather than only sharing a YouTube link. Format for platform: long, horizontal videos for YouTube; short, vertical clips for TikTok, Instagram Reels, and YouTube Shorts.

Always include a clear call to action in the video and video description: link to your author site and mailing list, a pinned comment with a booking or buy link, and captions or a transcript for accessibility and search.

Exercise—Set up your author YouTube channel. Explore the various settings and read the help files and tutorials.

Pinterest and Instagram

These two social media platforms are centered on images. If the topic of your book or your genre lends itself to being portrayed visually, then these, and similar ones, will work well for you.

They seem to be popular for recipes, hobbies, coloring books, art, photography, and any other subject that can be graphically portrayed.

Whatever you post will be reposted all over the web by potentially hundreds of thousands of people. If you post the uncolored coloring pages directly from your coloring books, you'll find people stealing them rather than buying your books.

Unless you purchase a third-party tool, you'll need to use a smartphone or similar device to post photos and images to Instagram. For an author, posting photos of the creative process, interviews, book signings, and activities can be successful. Keep your smartphone handy, and if something in your environment seems pertinent, then snap a photo and upload it to Instagram.

For Pinterest, photos and images must be added one at a time from a computer or from your smartphone and similar devices.

Both visual social networks require constant attention to be successful. For example, on Pinterest, you need to pin 20 to 50 images every day at different times. Pinning that many images all at once will not be nearly as successful.

Exercise–If you haven't already, create your Instagram and Pinterest accounts.

BookTok

I don't use BookTok myself, but I know authors who've had books take off there with no paid promotion and minimal following. The platform is real and it works — mostly for fiction, romance, YA, and thriller, but nonfiction can break through too if the content is genuinely useful or the author has a strong personality on camera.

BookTok runs on short vertical videos — 15 to 60 seconds, emotional, fast, and authentic. The first three seconds either hook someone or lose them. Polished production doesn't matter much; genuine reaction and personality do. The content that works best tends to be book reactions, personal recommendations with a specific emotional pitch, themed lists ("if you liked X, read this"), cover reveals, or behind-the-scenes glimpses of the writing process.

The audience skews younger — Gen Z and younger millennials — and is heavy on genre fiction. If your book fits that world, BookTok is worth experimenting with. If you write nonfiction business books, it's probably not your primary channel, but a short clip about a counterintuitive idea from your book can still find an audience.

Use current sounds and trending hashtags (#BookTok, #BookRec, #BookRecommendations). Post your profile link to your author site or email list, not just your Amazon page. If you build any momentum, post daily or close to it in the early stages to feed the algorithm. Once you have a rhythm, you can pull back to three or four times a week.

Exercise—Search BookTok for a book in your genre and watch ten videos. Notice what hooks you in the first three seconds and what makes you keep watching. Then watch ten more from authors directly. That's your template.

REDDIT

I don't use Reddit for promotion. I've watched it, and the culture is clear: Reddit users are allergic to obvious self-promotion, and they'll bury you publicly if you come in pushing your book. If you ignore that and post anyway, you'll be banned from the subreddit and possibly your account flagged.

That said, Reddit is genuinely useful for research. The subreddits r/books, r/writing, r/selfpublish, r/romancebooks, r/scifi, and dozens of genre-specific ones contain candid reader conversations about what they want, what they're tired of, what covers make them click, and what blurbs turn them off. Spend an hour reading threads in your genre and you'll learn more about your market than most courses will teach you.

If you want to participate beyond research, the only approach that works is to become a genuine member of the community first. Read the rules of every subreddit before posting — they vary a lot. Answer questions in your area of expertise without mentioning your book. Contribute something useful. Some subreddits have dedicated promotion days or AMA (Ask Me Anything) threads where authors are welcome. Use those when you've earned some standing in the community, not as your first move.

Budget about an hour a week if you use it at all. The research value alone is worth that.

Exercise—Find the subreddit for your book's genre or topic and spend 30 minutes reading the top posts from the past month. Don't post anything. Just read. Note what readers are asking for, complaining about, and recommending to each other. That's market research you can't buy.

AUTOMATION

Social media automation can save time, but it cannot replace real interaction. Use automation to schedule and recycle useful, evergreen content, not to pretend you are present. Schedule posts for the week, publish training videos or short lessons on a regular cadence, and let automation handle distribution. Reserve time each day for real responses, joining conversations, and answering messages.

Avoid automation that mimics people. Services that auto-follow, auto-like, or auto-comment attract low-quality followers and risk platform penalties. Deleted or banned tools have shown that bot-style automation is unreliable and dangerous. Use reputable schedulers and native platform tools to queue posts, then be the human who replies, thanks readers, and follows up.

Build an automation library of evergreen assets: short training clips, excerpts, testimonials, images, and simple graphics. Rotate those assets regularly, and add new material as you produce it. Track where clicks and signups come from so you can measure what the automation actually does for your list and sales.

Automation is a tool. Used wisely it reduces busywork and keeps your name visible. Used badly it creates noise, alienates readers, and damages credibility.

OUTSOURCING

Outsourcing tasks can free up your time, and it can work for parts of your social media. You can hire virtual assistants or professional firms to help.

Virtual assistants (VAs) are remote consultants found on platforms like Fiverr or through associations like the International Virtual Assistants Association (IVAA). VAs can handle repeatable, non-creative tasks. Do not expect them to do creative work, design content, or respond to comments. Their value is in managing routine, time-consuming actions.

For example, you can create Pinterest images and send them to a VA to schedule and post throughout the day. This maintains consistent activity without interrupting your writing. The best approach is to perform the task yourself first, then create a clear, step-by-step guide for your VA to follow.

Hiring professional social media firms can be expensive and risky. Quotes often start high, with long contracts and no guarantees. Even if affordable, these firms may struggle to create authentic content or interact effectively with your audience unless they deeply understand your market and message.

The best use of professionals is as advisors. Hire them to help develop campaign ideas, strategies, and overall design, then execute the daily tasks yourself or with a VA.

On platforms like LinkedIn and Facebook, there is no secure way to create sub-accounts for virtual assistants or other team members. Sharing your username and password violates their Terms and Conditions and poses a significant security risk. Granting someone direct access to your personal account can expose sensitive information, compromise your privacy, and potentially lead to unauthorized activity or account lockout.

Instead, use the built-in business tools these platforms offer. Facebook allows you to assign roles to people for Pages and Groups, granting specific permissions without sharing login credentials. LinkedIn provides similar administrative access for Company Pages. Always use these official features to manage team access, ensuring both security and compliance.

TYING IT ALL TOGETHER

Social media can become a time sink without generating significant sales. It is frustrating to spend hours daily on platforms only to see minimal returns. The goal is to find a balance that works for your brand and message without becoming a time trap.

The following sections summarize various platforms authors can use to reach readers, presented in order of general importance for most authors.

Author blog–Create and maintain a blog, preferably using WordPress under your own domain name. The blog is your home base, and everything should point back to it.

Email list–Create an email list, and actively pursue sign-ups, so that you can stay in touch with your readers.

YouTube Channel–YouTube videos are an excellent way to stay in contact and update your readers at a relatively low cost in time and money. You can create a video in a short time using a smartphone or webcam on your desktop or laptop, which can be posted to your blog and social media. Producing a video a week, or two a month, doesn't take a lot of time and keeps your readers engaged.

Facebook–Facebook is the most important social media platform for engaging with readers because virtually everyone is on Facebook every day, several times a week, or at least once a month. In fact, most people have Facebook installed on their desktops, cell phone, tablet, and everything else they own.

Create a Facebook page for you as an author and then another one for each of your major efforts–perhaps your most significant book or two, and your book series. Use these to stay in contact with your readers, as well as posting your YouTube videos and blog articles on each page.

LinkedIn–Create a LinkedIn profile, ensure it is professional and that it shows your career progression and how you became an author. Once you get the profile created, you don't need to spend a lot of time on LinkedIn. Half an hour a week is more than enough time to post a few status updates, add a picture, comment on a few things, and make a change here or there.

X–Create an X account, and post links to any articles that you write on your blog, any videos that you post to your YouTube channel, and anything important that you add to your Facebook pages.

Make sure your X handle is printed on all your written materials and stationary, on the contact page of your blog, and everywhere else visible to your readers.

Don't spend a lot of time with X, just post things that interest your audience and engage with your followers occasionally.

Pinterest and Instagram–If your topic lends itself to visual portrayals, such as recipe or coloring books, then you should use Pinterest and Instagram to promote your works. As with all other social media platforms, post for engagement, not for its own sake.

For example, if you publish coloring books, then you might post colored images of each page to your Pinterest and Instagram accounts.

Goodreads–Goodreads is an important social media platform for authors, but it's one of the most difficult to use effectively. Of all the various platforms, this is the one that tolerates self-promotion by authors the least. The best strategy is to create your author profile on Goodreads, and from that point on, forget you are an author and just take part in the conversations as a reader of other people's books. Eventually your books will get discovered by popular reviewers, which will cause increased sales.

BookTok, TikTok's book community–Create short, vertical videos that hook fast. Show a scene, a striking line, a reaction, a cover reveal, or a behind-the-scenes moment. Use current sounds and hashtags, keep clips punchy, and put a clear call to action in your bio that links to your author site or list. Post often while you build momentum–daily or several times a week–then drop to focused sessions of 15–30 minutes, three times a week once you have a rhythm.

Quora–Build a Quora profile that states your expertise and links to your author site. Answer targeted questions in your niche with useful, substantial responses. Avoid hard selling; let value and credibility do the work, and include a short author bio with links. Spend 30–60 minutes a week answering 2–5 careful questions and track which answers drive traffic.

Reddit–Find and follow a few subreddits that match your genre. Read the rules, engage genuinely, and contribute before you promote. Reddit rewards honest, long-form conversation; overt promotion often gets removed. Use Reddit for feedback, niche conversations, and occasional AMAs. Budget about an hour a week across two to three communities and prioritize relationship-building over broadcast posts.

MARKETING IS NOT OPTIONAL

An author I interviewed was direct about this: develop your marketing plan before you finish writing. Art is your passion, but it's also a business. You're an artistic entrepreneur. You can master the craft of writing, but if you can't get that book in front of your target audience, it doesn't matter how well you write.

Know your genre. Know who typically reads it. Know who your competition is. Then ask: how can you market in a way that stands out? In self-publishing especially, a lot of books are poorly formatted, full of errors, and don't come across as professional. Get the product right first, then figure out how to reach the people who want it. And know your story — what's unique about you, what you bring that nobody else does, and why readers should pay attention right now.

Market the Message, Not the Book

One of the better marketing insights I've encountered came from an author whose book became an international bestseller in a short period of time. Her approach: don't promote yourself or the book. Promote the message. People don't want to know what the book is — they want to know what it can do for them. Focus on outcomes and deliverables. That's the pitch.

She also started promoting before the book came out. Not a single big announcement on launch day, but a steady drip of content — ideas, concepts, excerpts — so that by the time the book was available, people were already interested and waiting. This is the opposite of the standard approach of finishing the book and then figuring out how to market it. Start earlier than you think you need to.

The other thing worth knowing before you start marketing: what is the objective behind the book? For many nonfiction authors, the book is not the end product — it's the credential that leads to coaching, speaking, workshops, or consulting. If that's true for you, your marketing should reflect it. You're not selling a book, you're demonstrating expertise that leads somewhere else. Know what that destination is and market toward it.

Marketing Realities for New Authors

A question new authors ask constantly: can I just pay someone to do the marketing? You can, but a self-publishing coach I interviewed is direct about this: for a new author with no prior awareness, you'll be wasting your money. A hired marketer can amplify existing momentum.

They cannot create it from nothing. Learn the marketing environment yourself first.

Her practical advice: set up a solid website — it doesn't need to be fancy, a clean WordPress site works fine — and make it the hub that everything points back to. Put an email collection system on it so you can reach readers directly when you have something new. For social media, pick one or two platforms you actually enjoy and stick with them. Don't try to do everything. Doing one thing consistently beats doing five things sporadically every time.

She also noted a tone calibration most new authors get wrong: there's a balance between being apologetic about your book and being too aggressive. You have to earn your standing and demonstrate your value before you can promote confidently. Readers can feel the difference between an author who is proud of what they've made and one who is pushing because they need the sale.

Be Everywhere

A self-published novelist I interviewed described her approach to promotion this way: people tell her she is everywhere. Conferences, speaking at conferences, local book fairs, social media, paid advertising, co-promotion with other authors, bookshop events, signings. She once did a book signing at a bank — entertaining people waiting in the queue with stories about murder and mayhem from her books. She found something to say wherever she could find an audience.

Her principle on timing: the best time to start promoting your book is right now. Not at launch. Now. If you haven't started writing yet, start promoting. If you have nine books and haven't done any promotion, start promoting. Tell people you're writing a book — they'll hold you accountable. When she announced her first book, people immediately asked where they could buy it. She hadn't written anything yet. That accountability helped her finish it.

TIME

Wow, that sure seems overwhelming, doesn't it?

It can feel overwhelming. Building an author platform is a long game. It will not happen overnight, in a month, or even in a year.

Start with a blog and an email list. Once those are working, add the social platforms that match your audience and your strengths. If you live on Facebook, begin there after your site and list. If you enjoy video, set up a YouTube channel and have at it.

Remember your primary mission: write and publish books and use social media as a tool to support that work. After you set up profiles, pages, and groups, limit active social time to under an hour a day. Batch tasks, schedule posts, and reserve that hour for replies, brief posting, and scanning for opportunities so social media does not become a time sink.

CONCLUSIONS

Build your platform early and maintain it consistently. A blog, an email list, and a few social media channels you actually use are all you need. The goal is to give readers a way to find you and stay connected. Keep it manageable or it will eat your writing time.

Chapter 7: Your Author Blog

I launched thewritingking.com in 2015, right after leaving The Ghost Publishing to start my own ghostwriting company. I built it myself in WordPress. It was primitive — a front page, an about section, a contact form, and a handful of articles. I had no idea what I was doing with it at first, and it showed.

That site has generated several hundred thousand dollars in business. Some clients found me directly through search. Others found me through a referral or a book and used the site to decide whether I was credible enough to hire. Both of those are reasons you need a blog. It isn't a direct sales tool — you probably won't make money from the blog itself — but it is the thing that closes the deal when someone is deciding whether to trust you.

My biggest mistake was making it too broad. I wrote about everything — dozens of subjects, scattered across whatever I felt like covering at the time. It took years to realize that a blog without focus is harder to find in search and harder for visitors to make sense of. I recently trimmed about 20% of the posts to tighten the site around what I actually do. Don't make the same mistake. Pick your lane early and stay in it.

Don't overthink the platform choice. I use WordPress on SiteGround and recommend it — it's flexible, widely supported, and you own everything. But plenty of successful authors use whatever blog builder came bundled with their hosting plan, or just set up a Wix site and get on with it. The platform matters far less than whether you actually publish to it consistently.

If you're starting from scratch and want a simple path: pick SiteGround for hosting, install WordPress, choose a clean free theme, and start writing. If the technical side of WordPress genuinely puts you off, Wix is fine. What isn't fine is spending three weeks comparing platforms instead of publishing your first post.

Why You Must Have a Blog

A blog should be your home base. Use it to publish articles about you and your work, post photos, and link to videos and other content.

Buy a personalized domain and email address. Many authors use their own name, for example richardlowe.com, while others use a business or book-series name.

If you do not want WordPress, you can create a simple blog on services such as Wix, Web.com, or Blogger and point your domain to that site. Domain forwarding is simple in concept: if your blog is damiansmith.web.com, buy damiansmith.com and set the registrar to forward it to damiansmith.web.com. Your registrar's help desk can walk you through it.

I host my sites on SiteGround and find it stable and fast. Hosting costs vary by plan and promotions; expect a modest first-year price that often includes a free domain, with higher renewal rates after the promotional period ends.

Running a blog is necessary if you want to build an author brand and increase income. You probably will not earn much directly from the blog but keeping it updated gives readers a place to learn about you, your books, upcoming plans, and to join your email list.

Do not use social media as your home base because you do not control the platform. You can lose a page or audience for policy violations, security breaches, or other platform changes.

If possible, pay for professional hosting and run WordPress. If you do not know how, hire someone or trade services with someone who does WordPress work. Initially you only need a front page, an about section, a contact page, and a few articles.

Use paid hosting so your content belongs to you. Free hosts can disappear; for example, GeoCities hosted millions of sites and was shut down by Yahoo in October 2009, causing many sites to vanish. Most hosts include email, but some restrict features or charge extra. Back up your site, enable SSL, and keep plugins and themes updated.

Post at least once a week if you can. Regular posts keep readers engaged and help grow your email list.

In summary, learn to create a blog and keep it current. Buy a domain, invest in reliable hosting, and use WordPress if you want full control and portability.

Domain Name

When you create your blog, get a domain name to go with it. Many hosts include a free domain for the first year when you buy hosting but offers vary.

Buy a custom domain whether you plan to wrestle with WordPress. A custom domain lets you use the same address in your books and promo materials and makes it easier to move your site later. If you use a hosted subdomain instead and then move, you will need to update every reference in your books, social profiles, and marketing.

Pick a domain that reinforces your brand and is easy to spell. Short, memorable names and a matching .com are best when available. Check trademark conflicts and make sure matching social handles are free.

A domain can be used for email, for example rich@thewritingking.com, but you must set up email hosting or use an email service provider. Domain registration alone does not create mailboxes; most hosts or third-party services can provide them. Set up MX records and authentication (SPF, DKIM, DMARC) so your mail does not get flagged as spam.

Once your blog, email, and domain are live, put the domain on business cards, invoices, letterhead, and email signatures. Everything should point back to your blog as your home base.

If you later move hosts, use proper site migration steps and 301 redirects to preserve links and search traffic. Consider domain privacy, enable auto-renew to avoid accidental loss, and get SSL for your site.

For an author brand example, a site and domain like thewritingking.com match the blog name, the brand, and email, which makes marketing consistent and professional.

The front page of your blog is vital, and the section that is "above the fold" (the top of the page that is visible on the screen) is the most important part of that.

On the image below, the sidebar is the white ribbon box at the top. This typically contains a menu (a way to choose where to go in the site), your logo, and a link to your signup form.

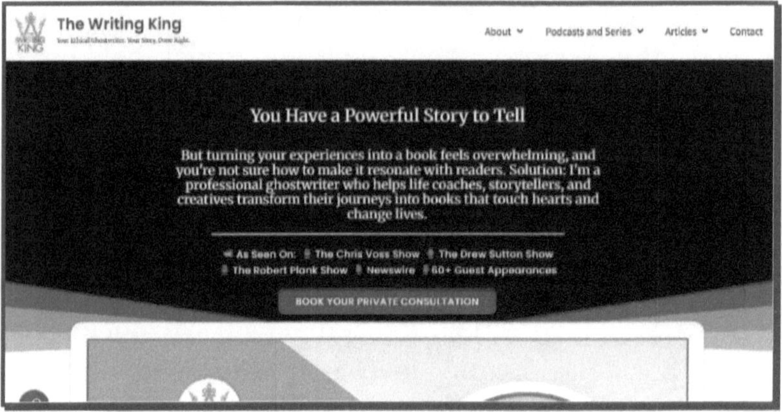

Keep your front page simple and easy to navigate; less clutter is better.

Include your picture and links to all your books or series above the fold. Visitors want to see you and your work first.

Ensure colors, fonts, and style project your desired image. Your blog must also be mobile-responsive, adapting smoothly to different screen sizes so it looks good and functions well on phones and tablets.

About Page

The About page tells readers about you or your company. It is the long version of your author biography, usually written in the third person as if someone else is introducing you. Include a few photos or drawings so readers can see who you are.

Place a clear call to action near the top of the page and again at the end of the bio. Use a short prompt such as "Join my newsletter", "Browse my books", or "Contact me" and link the button to the appropriate signup form, store page, or contact page. Make the action obvious and easy to complete.

Keep navigation consistent: the menu on the About page should match the rest of the site so visitors never wonder where to go next.

Spend time making your About page excellent; it will be one of your blog's most visited pages.

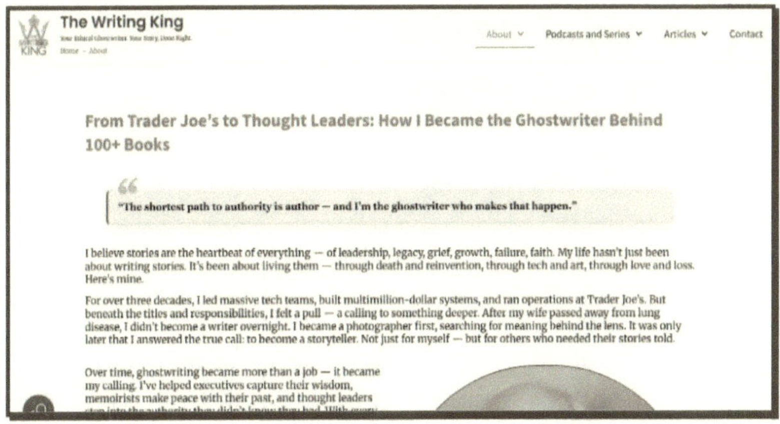

You must include a contact page on your blog. This is how people get ahold of you.

Use a form to collect their email address, name, and a message. Don't ask them for more information than that. All you need is a way to get back to them and their message.

Also, don't put your email address, phone number, or home address out on the web. Let them contact you through your form. Putting your private information on your contact form makes it available to spammers and scammers.

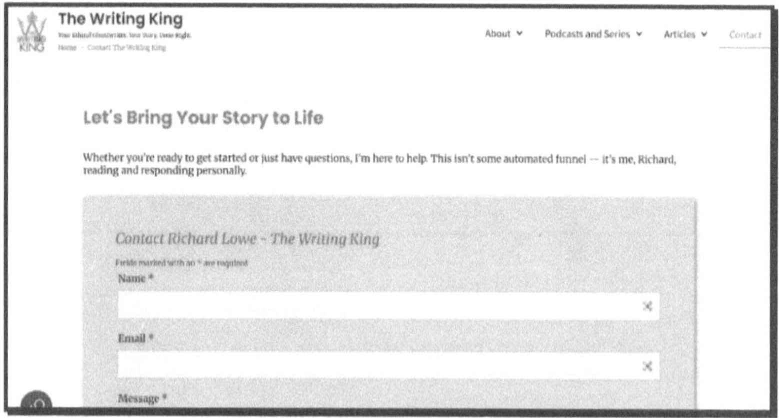

MEDIA PAGE

The purpose of a media page is to provide members of the press, podcasters, producers, and others with the information they need for articles or shows.

Keep your media page simple to begin with, and add to it over time as you gain experience and credentials. Ensure it is accurate, promotes you well, and is easy to navigate.

Include:

- A biography written in the third person.
- Several professional photos (up to 4).
- An introduction to be used for speaking engagements.
- The answers to a few sample interview questions.
- The contact information for your publicist, if appropriate.
- A list of your books, articles and other materials.

It's common for the media page to be one of the most heavily accessed pages on a blog.

RECOMMENDED PLUGINS

WordPress allows you to install many applications called plugins, each modifying your blog's behavior. Tens of thousands of plugins are available for every conceivable function, and a few are especially useful for an author's blog.

This book will not detail these plugins. This list includes those I find most useful, so you can investigate and use them if they appeal to you.

Antispam Bee–Protect your forms from spam.

Ninja Forms–Beautiful forms.

Wordfence Security–Secure your website.

WordPress Books Gallery–An excellent book gallery page.

XML Sitemap Generator for Google–Generate site maps. This is needed for Google indexing.

Once you discover plugins, it is tempting to install dozens because they make it easy to add features and change your site. Think of them as building blocks for blogs.

Resist the urge to install more than a dozen, or at most two dozen. Each plugin can affect performance, security, and reliability. Avoid plugins that are not tested on your WordPress version or that have several recent negative reviews. Check last-updated dates, active-install counts, and support threads before you install.

Back up your site, use a staging site to test changes, and keep plugins updated. If you do not understand WordPress, hire someone who does or take a course on a platform such as Udemy. You do not need plugins to get started.

CONCLUSIONS

Your blog is the most important component of your author platform. It gives you a home on the internet and a reference point for readers and other interested people.

Keep your blog updated and post to it often, at least once a week. Everything about you, your books, and your series should be available to visitors.

WordPress is an excellent platform for your blog because it is flexible. Many themes (blueprints for how your blog looks) and plugins are available, allowing you to customize it to your exact needs.

Once your blog is up and running, even in a simplified version, the next step for your author platform is to create and build your email list.

Chapter 8: Your Email List

I\'ve used just about every email service out there. For years I had a list of a couple thousand people and did almost nothing with it. Not because I was lazy — because I genuinely didn\'t know what to do with it. I had the list, I sent the occasional newsletter, and nothing happened. No book sales spike, no ghostwriting inquiries, nothing. It sat there collecting digital dust.

My biggest mistake was buying leads. It sounds like a reasonable shortcut — pay for a list of people who are supposedly interested in your topic and skip the slow work of building organically. It doesn\'t work. Bought leads don\'t know who you are, didn\'t ask to hear from you, and will ignore, delete, or mark you as spam. I wasted time and money on lists that generated nothing and damaged my sender reputation in the process.

Now I\'m building it the right way — through my blog and my book funnel. People who find thewritingking.com through search or referral, or who read one of my books and follow the link in the back matter, are actually interested in what I do. Those subscribers open emails. That\'s the list you want. It\'s slower to build and completely worth it.

LEAD MAGNETS

Create a lead magnet to attract people to your email list. A lead magnet is a free, valuable item you give away to entice subscriptions. Examples include a PDF, checklist, interview, video, or sample chapter.

A coloring-book list might use an eight-page sample of coloring book pages. If you wrote a book about LinkedIn, give away a LinkedIn setup checklist. Fiction authors often give away a first chapter or two or an entire short book.

After you create the lead magnet, set up a signup form on your blog that collects only name and email. Deliver the magnet automatically via your autoresponder so subscribers get it immediately. Keep file sizes reasonable and provide mobile-friendly formats. Use a clear subject line and a landing or thank-you page that confirms delivery. On the signup form, include a short promise about email frequency and content to manage expectations and improve signups.

Mention the free product in your books, both front and back matter, and link to a dedicated signup page. For print, use a short URL [15] or QR code to reduce typos. Consider offering a lead magnet that previews the value of your regular emails to boost retention.

Exercise–Think about your book. What kind of lead magnet would make sense to get people to subscribe to your mailing list? Think about:

- For a novel, a short prequel would be a great freebie and will also set the scene for your novel.
- For non-fiction, a checklist, a video tutorial, or even a Rolodex of contacts.

---

[15] Be careful with URL shorteners. Spam filters often mark emails containing these short URLs as spam.

What kind of freebie makes sense for your book or book series?

SERVICES

To automate your email list, you need to choose an autoresponder service. Some of the best services are listed below.

Kit (previously known as ConvertKit)–Kit focuses specifically on creators and authors. It provides strong automation features, subscriber tagging, and landing page builders. The interface remains simpler than MailChimp's bloated current version, and pricing stays competitive for growing lists.

Aweber–Aweber is a top-of-the-line autoresponder provider. They also have a free version available and provide paid upgrade options. They can handle lists of all sizes, but their options are more complex and more suitable for advanced users.

Exercise–Visit each of the sites above and read the descriptions thoroughly. Which of them appears to be best for you? Sign up for a free account on Kit and experiment with the options available.

Once you select a service, read its documentation thoroughly and start creating your autoresponder sequences.

An autoresponder sequence is a series of email messages sent to each subscriber in a specific order and timeframe.

For example, look at the list below:

- Immediately after subscribing, send a welcome message.
- One day later: introduce yourself with a brief biography.
- Three days after that, send an article describing why you became an author.
- Three days after that, send a list of your books.
- And so forth–

Autoresponders handle delivery automatically. Create the lead magnet and the email messages. You can build as many messages as you want and set intervals between them–hours, days, weeks, or months.

Send content that builds a relationship and delivers consistent value. Treat email like your social posts but with deeper, more useful material. Examples: a course split into ten lessons, sample chapters or snippets for fiction, or a periodic free coloring page for coloring-book lists. Segment your list and tailor sequences to reader interest for better results.

Avoid giving away too much for free. You train your list by what you send, and habitual giveaways can reduce purchases. Use freebies sparingly and with a clear purpose. Track open and click rates, test subject lines, and measure conversions.

Your email list keeps you connected to readers who asked to hear from you and are therefore more likely to engage. Use double opt-in where appropriate, include a working unsubscribe link, and follow relevant laws and privacy rules. Add a clear call to action in each message and limit the promotional-to-value ratio so subscribers expect value and occasional offers.

Exercise–Kit has some great tutorials on how to do email campaigns. Look through them to get more information on how you can use this tool.

OCCASIONAL MESSAGES

Besides your automated (canned) messages, you should also occasionally send broadcast emails to your list to inform them about current events or news.

For example:

- When you publish a new book.
- If you are giving a speech or a book signing.
- If you are featured in a media event such as a television interview.
- If you win an award or are highly honored.

- And other similar events.

Do not send unscheduled broadcast emails too often. Once a month is a good baseline. Weekly messages can be too frequent for many audiences, although some niches accept weekly contact.

Tell subscribers what to expect when they sign up, and adjust frequency based on open rates, click-throughs, and unsubscribe rates. Segment your list so only relevant groups get extra messages, and keep broadcasts focused, valuable, and clearly labeled as updates or promotions.

Maintain a healthy promotional-to-value ratio, for example one promotional message for every two or three value emails. Run re-engagement campaigns for inactive subscribers to clean your list and protect deliverability.

Example cadences:

- Fiction authors: monthly newsletter, additional launch promos and occasional limited offers.
- Nonfiction authors/coaches: biweekly or weekly tips if you provide high-value content.
- Authors with frequent launches: increase frequency in the lead-up to a launch, then revert to baseline.

Track performance: monitor open rate, click-through rate, conversion rate, unsubscribe rate, and deliverability. A/B test subject lines and calls to action and use results to refine cadence and content.

Your email list is a marketing tool to stay in contact with readers and keep them engaged with your brand. It is not an advertising channel in the usual sense. Affiliate marketers often use their lists for heavy advertising and may send daily promotions tied to webinars or product funnels.

Webinars can teach useful things, but their primary purpose is often to sell products. Expect the presenter to build a case that the product is worth buying.

Use your author list to build engagement so readers buy your books and other products. One email per week is a solid baseline. Up to two per week can work if you consistently deliver value and your audience expects that cadence. Fewer than one message every two weeks risks losing engagement.

Send occasional manual broadcasts for timely items such as a new book or an event. Do not include those one-off messages in your evergreen autoresponder sequence.

Too many messages will alienate readers. They will ignore, delete, or mark your mail as spam. Track open rates, click rates, unsubscribe rates, and spam complaints, and adjust frequency based on those metrics. Segment your list so only relevant groups receive extra messages. Maintain a healthy promotional-to-value ratio so subscribers expect value and occasional offers.

Use double opt-in where appropriate, include a working unsubscribe link in every message, and follow email laws such as CAN-SPAM and GDPR. Run a re-engagement campaign every six to twelve months to clean inactive subscribers and protect deliverability.

Consider a promotional-to-value guideline of one promotional message for every two or three value messages.

Keep your email list simple. A weekly autoresponder message and the occasional announcement is enough for most authors. More complexity means less time writing. That's a bad trade.

Chapter 9: Legal Concerns

I am not a lawyer, and the information in this section is for general guidance only. For specific advice on any of these topics, consult an attorney and conduct your own research.

Most self-published authors don't think about legal issues until something bites them. That's a mistake. You don't need a law degree, but you do need to understand the basics: copyright, trademarks, defamation, and permissions. Get those wrong and you can lose your book listing, eat a cease-and-desist, or end up in a lawsuit.

Here's what you need to know. Copyright protects your work the moment you create it—but registering it in the United States gives you better legal options if someone steals it. Trademarks protect brand identifiers, and using them incorrectly in a title or cover can get you into trouble with corporate legal departments faster than you'd expect (I watched this happen to a client). Defamation covers false statements that damage someone's reputation—libel when written, slander when spoken—and fiction doesn't automatically protect you if a character is recognizable. And anything you didn't create yourself—images, music, quotes, cover art—needs written permission before you use it.

This chapter covers each of these areas. For anything involving real money or real risk, talk to a publishing lawyer. An hour of their time is cheaper than the alternative.

COPYRIGHT

People work hard to create graphics, stories, website designs, software, and other original work. In most countries, including the United States, copyright protects those works automatically as soon as they are fixed in a tangible form. You do not need to register to have copyright, but registration in the United States gives you stronger legal remedies and makes enforcement easier. Keep records of drafts and creation dates and register when you can.

The copyright owner controls the right to reproduce, distribute, display, and create derivative works. You can grant others limited rights, for example to display an image or adapt a book for film but do so in writing.

Using someone's images, text, music, video, or other material without permission is copyright infringement except where a legal exception applies, such as fair use.

Infringement can give rise to civil liability and, in some willful or commercial cases, criminal penalties. [16]

If you want to use excerpts from another work, request permission from the copyright owner and get a written license specifying scope, duration, territory, and any fee. Do not assume credit is enough. Many creators will agree to reuse for credit or payment but confirm terms in writing.

Consider alternatives when possible: use public domain material, content under a permissive Creative Commons license, licensed stock content, or original material you create yourself. Keep records of permissions, drafts, and registration receipts to prove ownership and dates of creation.

When you do get permission, get it in writing and be specific. A vague "sure, go ahead" email won't protect you if things go sideways later. Spell out exactly what you're using, in what formats, for how long, and what you're paying (if anything). Keep a copy of every agreement in your project folder. If you're going international or doing anything with significant commercial value, talk to a publishing lawyer before you publish, not after.

----

[16] While copyright infringement is primarily a civil matter, it *can* have criminal penalties in cases of willful infringement for commercial advantage or private financial gain. So, it's not *always* non-criminal.

Some examples of behavior that violate copyright law in the United States are:

Taking images from newsgroups. Just because something has been copied to a newsgroup, regardless of whether the copy was made by the copyright owner or someone else, does not mean that the copyright has been given up.

Using articles and images from other websites. Again, this is illegal unless explicit permission is given, or the item in question is in the public domain. However, you can link to anything on the web without permission; linking does not violate any United States laws.

Scanning images from magazines and books. This is illegal as you are making a copy (a scan) of a copyrighted work.

Changing an image and claiming it as your own. Copyright protects derivations of works as well.

AI tools do not remove copyright obligations. You may link freely, but you must not copy or scan articles or images from other sites or print sources without permission. Uploading third-party images into AI tools or changing an image and claiming it as your own can still violate copyright because derivative works are protected. Use only public domain or properly licensed images, secure written permission for copyrighted material, and keep records of licenses and releases.

The following are acceptable under the U.S. copyright laws.

Including a few brief quotes from a book in a review. This is acceptable under fair use laws. Include a citation to give credit to the source.

Reprinting or copying parts from a confirmed public domain novel.

Asking and getting reprint permission. If you get permission from the copyright owner or their legal agent, you are fine. Be sure to get permission in writing.

Reading an article about cheese puffs and writing your own article about cheese puffs. Copyright protects creative works, and any derivations made from them, but not ideas or concepts.

When in doubt, ask permission. If you are denied permission or cannot get it, then don't use the material.

And always cite your sources.

FAIR USE

To include quotes from another author's work, U.S. copyright law provides a limited exception called fair use. Fair use can allow quoting or excerpting copyrighted material for purposes such as commentary, criticism, news reporting, scholarship, education, and parody. Fair use is decided case by case under the four statutory factors in 17 U.S.C. §107:

- The purpose and character of the use (including whether it is transformative)
- The nature of the work.
- How much was used.
- The effect on the original work's market.

A few brief quotes in a review or research paper often qualify, but copying substantial portions, scanning magazine photos, or reposting full website pages usually does not.

Attribution is good practice but does not guarantee fair use. Obtain written permission when in doubt and be aware that some uses can raise other legal issues such as rights of publicity or contract restrictions.

For example, if you write an article about the quality of the movie "The Mummy Returns", you could use brief quotes from the film to illustrate your point. However, if you included the entire script (or significant portions of it), then that would be a copyright violation.

Include a reference (citation) to the original source material. This gives readers the opportunity to look at the source document for additional information. You add to your credibility by showing you have done your research.

To further illustrate, the following would most likely be covered under fair use:

- Including brief quotes from published papers in research papers.
- Reviewing a book and including a few quotes to illustrate your point.

- Reviewing a book and including quotes from other critics to reinforce your point.

The following would most likely be copyright violations:

- Including without permission several pages of material from another research paper.
- Wholesale copying of pages from a website to your book.
- Scanning photographs of Heather Locklear from Cosmopolitan and using them in your book or website.

TRADEMARKS

Trademarks are words, phrases, or graphics reserved by businesses or people for brand identification. They are typically product names, logos, slogans, and similar branding elements.

A service mark is a type of trademark used to identify services rather than goods. In practice people often call both trademarks.

In the United States, you do not need to register a trademark to get basic rights. Use in commerce creates common-law rights. Registration with the USPTO is recommended because it gives nationwide priority, a presumption of ownership, the ability to sue in federal court, and the right to use the registered symbol ®.

Trademark rights arise from use, but registration strengthens enforcement. Owners must police their marks to avoid abandonment or genericide. That said, you may reference a trademark in a book if the use does not imply endorsement or cause confusion. Nominative fair use allows limited references to identify the trademarked product or service, provided you use only what is necessary and avoid suggesting sponsorship.

Be cautious with logos, product packaging, and merchandising rights, which often require permission. Note that single book titles are rarely trademarkable as titles, while book series titles can be. Trademark rules and remedies vary by country, so confirm requirements for international use.

TRADEMARKS IN THE TEXT

There are a few areas that you need to be concerned about as a writer if you use trademarks.

Infringement–Trademark infringement is an unauthorized use of the mark that creates the likelihood of confusion about the product or services. For example, if a company created an airplane called Boeing, then the Boeing Corporation would likely demand that they stop using that name for their product.

Dilution–If you use a trademark generically, such as referring to 'photocopying' as a 'xeroxing', this dilutes the trademark because it makes it more generic instead of specific to the brand.

Defamation–This is falsely depicting a trademarked product or service in a negative light. For example, if you wrote a fiction story about Coca-Cola® killing people straight out of the bottle, you might get a sternly worded letter from that company. Here, it is better to use a fictional brand name to protect yourself.

The key is to use trademarks respectfully and with correct formatting. For example, if you reference eBay, spell and capitalize it exactly right (e.g., "eBay," not "Ebay").

Respectful use of trade or service marks in your book's body text should not cause problems. However, exercise caution on your book cover, title, subtitle, and series name. Using a trademark in these prominent locations can imply endorsement or affiliation, which is generally not allowed without explicit permission.

COPYRIGHT PAGE NOTICE

If you use trademarks in your book, add a short disclaimer on the copyright page. A simple, standard notice works well. We will discuss this further in Chapter 13.

TRADEMARKS IN THE BOOK TITLE

A ghostwriting client of mine faced disaster because he used a trademarked product name in his book title. A few months after publishing, he received a cease-and-desist order, had to unpublish the book, and republish it under a new title. Because of this, he lost dozens of four- and five-star reviews.

The risk with trademarks in titles is reader confusion about endorsement or affiliation. To protect their marks, companies often enforce rights through cease-and-desist letters and, in extreme cases, litigation.

Avoid using trademarks in your title, subtitle, or cover unless you have written permission. If you must reference a trademark, limit it to the body text, spell and capitalize the name exactly as the owner uses it, and do not use logos or brand artwork without a license.

Before publishing, search the web and trademark databases for the name and check the company's branding or trademark usage page for rules and contact information. If guidance is not available, contact the brand and get written permission that specifies scope, territory, duration, formats, and any fees. Keep the permission documents with your project files.

Changing a print book title often requires retiring the current edition and issuing a new one, which can break retailer links and remove reviews. Rules vary by retailer and country, so expect significant disruption if you must republish. For high-value or risky uses, get written clearance before publishing and consult a publishing or trademark attorney.

LIBEL AND SLANDER

Defamation is the act of making false statements about another person or entity that damage their reputation. Written defamation is libel; spoken defamation is slander.

As you write, whether fiction or nonfiction, avoid defaming any person, business, or brand. Portraying a recognizable person in an unwholesome way, such as alleging criminal acts, drug use, or affairs, can lead to a lawsuit. Changing only names does not protect you; if circumstances are recognizable, a person could still sue.

Truth is an absolute defense to defamation. If you state that Miss Betsy committed adultery, and it is true and provable, you have not defamed her. If she openly discussed the matter, you would likely be safe. Conversely, false allegations about a rock star or public figure can produce liability. Note that in the United States public figures face a higher burden. They generally must prove actual malice, meaning the statement was made knowing it was false or with reckless disregard for the truth.

In fiction, you can commit libel if characters and circumstances are recognizable even without explicit naming. To reduce risk, change multiple identifying details: appearance, location, habits, timeline, and names so the situation is not identifiable.

Defamation is typically a civil action. You cannot be jailed for writing something defamatory in most cases, but you can be sued and, if you lose, ordered to pay damages. Legal defense costs can be substantial even for meritless suits, so prevention is crucial. Follow journalistic standards when making factual claims: verify facts with multiple sources, keep notes, and document interviews and evidence.

Consider insurance. Errors and omissions insurance, also called professional liability insurance, can cover legal defense and settlements for claims such as plagiarism, copyright infringement, and defamation depending on the policy. I have E&O specifically for writing related issues that covers lawsuits for plagiarism, copyright infringement, defamation, and similar claims. Check any policy carefully for exclusions and limits.

E&O policies are described in detail in the next section.

If you plan to portray a real person negatively, ensure your statements are true and provable, or change the facts enough to prevent recognition and consult a lawyer before publishing.

ERRORS AND OMISSIONS INSURANCE

Errors and omissions insurance, often called E&O or media liability insurance, protects you against the cost of defending and resolving certain legal claims that arise from your writing.

For authors, this typically covers risks such as libel, slander, defamation, invasion of privacy, copyright and plagiarism claims, and some types of errors in factual work. E&O policies pay legal defense costs, settlements, and judgments up to the policy limits when a covered claim is made.

I have E&O specifically for writing-related issues that covers lawsuits for plagiarism, copyright infringement, defamation, and similar claims.

Most E&O policies work on a claims-made basis: the claim has to be made while the policy is active, and the policy has a retroactive date that determines how far back it covers. Pay attention to that date—if you publish something risky before the retroactive date, you're not covered. Also check whether legal defense costs come out of your coverage limit or are paid on top of it. That distinction matters a lot when legal fees start piling up.

E&O typically covers libel, defamation, copyright infringement, plagiarism, and invasion of privacy. What it usually doesn't cover: criminal acts, deliberate falsification, trademark disputes (unless specifically included), and cybersecurity breaches. Read the exclusions carefully before you buy. If you write about public figures, do investigative nonfiction, or publish widely, consider higher limits.

A few practical rules: notify your insurer the moment someone threatens a claim—delayed notice can void coverage. Never admit fault or negotiate with a claimant on your own. And before publishing, get written permissions for third-party content, document your sources, and check your cover and title for anything that could imply endorsement. Even a meritless lawsuit can cost tens of thousands in legal fees to defend. That's what E&O is for.

When shopping for a policy, find a broker who knows publishing. Ask specifically about retroactive date options, whether defense costs are inside or outside the limits, and whether trademark claims are covered. Get a multi-year policy if you can.

For ghostwriters, this insurance is particularly critical. As a ghostwriter, you often work with clients who may provide you with information, stories, or even existing content that could inadvertently contain defamatory statements, infringe on copyrights, or violate privacy rights.

Even if the client provides the problematic material, you, as the writer, can still be named in a lawsuit. E&O insurance provides a vital layer of protection, covering your legal defense and potential damages, even if the fault ultimately lies with the client. It safeguards your professional reputation and financial stability against claims arising from content you create on behalf of others.

AI tools create new text, images, audio, and code, but using them doesn't erase your legal duties. Copyright still applies.

You face two main risks: First, if you feed copyrighted material into an AI tool without permission, you could be infringing. Second, the AI's output itself might infringe if it too closely copies or is based on copyrighted material used to train it.

Many AI companies train their models on content without explicit licenses, so the legal landscape is still shifting. Also, purely AI-generated works, without enough human input, might not get copyright protection in places like the U.S.

For authors and ghostwriters, the simple rules are to avoid uploading copyrighted images, text, or music into an AI tool unless you have written permission or a clear license.

Stick to public domain, Creative Commons (with proper terms), or licensed material for your inputs. Use AI models whose terms clearly allow your commercial use and save a copy of those terms.

Keep records of your prompts, the model used, the date, the provider's terms, and any sources you provided; this helps prove ownership and origin.

Treat AI outputs like any other third-party content: check them for similarity to existing works, and if something looks derivative, clear the rights.

Do not assume simply crediting the AI makes an infringing use legal. If you're doing anything high-risk—like adapting a living author's work, using a celebrity's likeness, or creating commercial assets from AI outputs–get written permission or talk to a lawyer.

Consider E&O insurance that specifically covers AI risks.

CONCLUSIONS

Do not let others steal your work or profit from it. Respect other people's copyrights and seek permission when you want to reuse their material.

Do not publish untrue or malicious statements about anyone. Verify factual claims and avoid identifiable portrayals that could be defamatory.

Respect trademarks and service marks by following the brand owner's usage rules and avoiding implied endorsement or affiliation. Correct spelling and formatting do not eliminate trademark risk.

If you have concerns about your manuscript, consult an attorney.

Chapter 10: The Book Cover

Your book's cover is the most critical element for converting browsers into buyers. Many readers make their initial decision to engage with a book based solely on its cover. A poorly designed cover will significantly hinder sales.

The cover must convey the book's content with clarity and impact. The interplay of fonts, colors, graphics, and the arrangement of all components either draws readers in or pushes them away.

Genre conventions are essential. A romance novel's cover will differ vastly from a science fiction or historical nonfiction book. Meeting your audience's expectations is key to reaching your intended readership.

This cover was commissioned on Fiverr. I selected a designer based on samples and reviews, supplied the title and brand direction, and paid extra for commercial rights. The designer provided several drafts and two rounds of revisions before we settled on the final layout.

It is critical that the title be large enough on the cover to be read clearly when the image appears as a thumbnail, since thumbnails are the primary thing readers see in store listings.

Designing a good cover is both science and art, and unless you have formal training in graphic design it is usually best to hire a skilled designer to create it.

For Unlikely Heroes I used Claude.ai to craft a precise image prompt, generated the background in Leonardo.ai, then added type and final polish in Paint Shop Pro 2023 (a much less expensive option than Adobe Photoshop with similar functionality).

Fiverr.com is an excellent resource for finding book cover designers. Always check their reviews and sample portfolios to assess their skill.

I've used several different cover designers on Fiverr. Sometimes they produce good or even excellent covers; other times, they are poorly crafted. I found some of these "people" subcontract to hire multiple artists. This can cause uneven quality from the same gig.

Ensure you secure commercial licensing for the cover from the designer and for all images used. Many Fiverr gigs offer commercial licenses as an add-on, but a quick email to the artist often results in a custom gig that includes the license at no extra charge.

Even with commercial rights from the cover designer, you must verify the legal use of all images. The safest approach is to source images yourself from reputable stock photo sites and provide them to the designer, ensuring you hold the necessary commercial rights. Always read the fine print. Never use images found randomly online; public availability does not grant usage rights.

Most gigs include several revisions; ensure at least two are offered. Covers frequently require multiple adjustments before reaching a satisfactory final version.

On Fiverr.com, expect to pay $5 to $25 for a high-quality, effective cover. Professional graphic designers outside of platforms like Fiverr typically charge $100 to $500 for a high-quality cover.

Keep a folder with gig URL/screenshots, invoice or license confirmation, stock receipts, model releases, and final master files.

Exercise–Go to Amazon.com and look at a dozen different books. Examine the covers closely. Do they want to make you look at or purchase the book?

MAKING COVERS YOURSELF

If you want to make your own book covers, Canva.com is a great place to start. Create an account and use their book cover template. They have pre-made ones for eBooks that works great. These covers are not as you'd get from a professional, but they are still good, and you can't beat the price (free).

If you want more control, buy editable cover templates in common formats such as PSD. These templates are widely available from marketplace sites and independent sellers.

Edit templates with Adobe Photoshop, Paint Shop Pro 2023, Affinity Photo, or the free editor GIMP. Some programs do not preserve every Photoshop layer or effect (Paint Shop Pro and GIMP commonly lose adjustment layers and layer styles, and Affinity can have trouble with smart objects), so test a sample template in your software before you buy.

There are several reputable places to buy covers or hire designers beyond Fiverr. Marketplaces with premade covers let you pick a finished design and have the text swapped, while designer marketplaces and studios offer custom work.

Prices and quality vary widely, so shop by portfolio and licensing terms rather than by price alone. Store your purchase receipts, license statements, and final master files with the project.

Useful sites and when to use them

- <u>BookCovers.com (formerly SelfPubBookCovers)</u>, premade covers, large catalog, cover removed after purchase.
- <u>Reedsy</u>, vetted professional designers for custom covers, higher cost but publisher-level quality.
- <u>Damonza</u>, design studio, full-service custom covers and packages.
- <u>99designs</u>, contest and direct hire options, good for exploring many concepts.
- <u>BookBaby</u>, full self-publishing service with in-house design.
- <u>Bookfly Design</u>, small studio for custom covers and interior work.
- <u>BookBrush</u>, author-focused tools for mockups, templates, and social assets.
- <u>GetPremades</u> and <u>BookCoverZone</u>, premade cover catalogs at budget-friendly prices.

One principle worth internalizing: before you do any significant marketing, have the best product possible. A self-publishing author I interviewed was direct about this — you can market to kingdom come, but if the product is poor, you won't get repeat buyers. Engage professional services — editing, proofreading, cover design — as your budget permits. Nobody can do everything to a professional standard by themselves. Figure out where your weaknesses are and hire for them.

A bad cover kills sales. If your book isn't moving, look at the cover first. Hire someone who knows what they're doing, check that the title reads clearly as a thumbnail, and don't be afraid to change it if it's not working.

Chapter 11: Metadata

Information about your book is called metadata. This includes the title, subtitle, author, other people who worked on your book (cover artist, editor, and so on), series, and ISBN number, among other things.

Before you publish your book, define and write down this information so you can easily enter it into KDP.

The significant metadata is described in the following sections.

If you're going to publish more than one book, or more than one edition of the same book, then consider defining an imprint (also known as a publishing company). This is just a name and has nothing to do with a real-world publishing company or entity. You do not need to incorporate or file a DBA (Doing Business As) legal document to define a publisher[17].

There are two things you'll need to do: come up with a name and purchase a block (preferably) of ISBNs.

The name you choose should reinforce your brand–which is the image you are trying to portray to the outside world–and be consistent across all your books.

Some authors use the imprint name as another way to enter keywords, so it is different for all their books. While not forbidden, this violates the purpose of the publisher name, which is to identify your publishing company.

For example, if you are publishing coloring books you might define an imprint of "Ron's Coloring Books" or if you are an artist you could use "Zen Art". The name is entirely up to you. Just make sure it's not a domain name, a trademark or the name of another book.

If you want to use a publisher name or imprint, you will need to purchase and assign ISBN numbers.

Do not use the ISBN, either free or for a fee, provided by KDP, Lulu, or other publishing company. You should use

---

[17] Although, of course, you can define a business if you want.

ISBNs that you purchase and assign to get the full benefit of using your own imprint.

Using an ISBN purchased and assigned by you, rather than one provided by a publishing platform, is crucial for maintaining full control and ownership over your book's identity. This ensures your chosen imprint is listed as the publisher in all industry databases, enhancing your brand, providing greater flexibility in distribution channels, and improving long-term portability and professional recognition for your work.

The imprint name shows up on your book page in the *Product Details* section, as in the example below ("The Writing King"). If you don't include one when you publish the book, it will show up as something like "Amazon Digital Services LLC".

Product Details

Series: Earn Money from Your Home
Paperback: 132 pages
Publisher: The Writing King (August 4, 2016)
Language: English
ISBN-10: 1943517363
ISBN-13: 978-1943517367
Product Dimensions: 6 x 0.3 x 9 inches
Shipping Weight: 1.6 ounces (View shipping rates and policies)
Average Customer Review: ☆☆☆☆☆ (25 customer reviews)
Amazon Best Sellers Rank: #93,948 in Books (See Top 100 in Books)
    #13 in Books > Computers & Technology > Internet & Social Media > **eBay**
    #92 in Books > Business & Money > Small Business & Entrepreneurship > **Home Based**

In addition, you should include the imprint name on the title page of each edition of your books. For eBooks, I include a link below the title to my publisher website so that my readers can visit to look at my other books and projects.

Exercise–Make a list of possible Imprint Names that promote the brand and image you want to portray. Look over the list and keep adding to it until you find a name that works for you.

ISBN

An ISBN, or International Standard Book Number, is commonly assigned to each edition and variation of a book. They are used by bookstores, libraries, and so forth to identify each specific title and edition.

The ISBN was not optional back in the days of traditional publishing and bookselling. If a book didn't have an ISBN, it would not be on the shelves of bookstores and libraries. Authors normally didn't have to deal with assigning them because this was done by publishers. With self-publishing, authors who write and publish their own books must take responsibility for deciding whether to use ISBNs and then purchasing them if needed.

There is some debate as to whether ISBNs are even necessary anymore, at least with electronic books such as those for the Kindle or the Nook. In fact, the ISBN is optional when publishing a book for Kindle because Amazon uses an internal number, called an ASIN, to identify your book.

For paperbacks, Amazon, under the KDP umbrella, will give you a free ISBN number if you choose. This shows your book as being published by Amazon, rather than by you.

If you decide to get your own ISBN numbers, you'll need to head on over to Bowker.com and purchase them[18]. You can purchase just one, which is very expensive, a block of ten, or a block of one hundred, which is the best deal commonly used by self-publishers.

If you publish more than one version of your book, for example an eBook (optionally), a paperback, and hardcover, then you'll need one ISBN number for each one. Also, if you republish the book as a new edition, then you must get a new ISBN number for it as well.

As you can see, if you publish a lot of books you could wind up going through quite a few ISBNs.

You have the option of purchasing ISBNs through your publisher, for example KDP, but if you're going to do that you may as well purchase your own directly from Bowker.com.

The website for Bowker.com can be a little intimidating to navigate. However, once you have gone through it once or twice, you'll find that it becomes friendlier. If you need help, Bowker has a customer service number at the top of their website, and they'll be happy to guide you through the process and explain what everything means.

There are several reasons why you may want or need to use your own ISBN numbers.

- If you want to sell your book to libraries or bookstores, you must use your own ISBNs.

---

[18] Bowker is the source of all ISBN numbers in the United States. For other countries, you'll need to find who provides the numbers.

- An ISBN along with a publisher name adds a certain amount of credibility to your publishing business. This raises you from being "merely" a self-publisher to being an honest to God publisher.
- If you want to sell your book on other retailers, such as Apple Books, you will need ISBNs.
- If you want your eBook to rank on Google, you'll need ISBNs to list the book in Bowker's *Books in Print* database.
- Some countries require ISBNs.

Exercise–Visit the Bowker website, create an account if you don't already have one, and read through the documentation.

PCN Number

For your paperback and hardcover versions, make the effort to acquire a PCN number. These numbers are what the United States Library of Congress uses to identify books, and the entire U.S. library system follows their lead.

In the United States, if you want your book to be acquired by libraries, you need to get a PCN number.

PCN numbers are free of charge, except that you will need to send a copy of the book to the Library of Congress once it is published.

Before submitting books to the PCN system, you'll need to get an ISBN number for each one at Bowker.com, as described in the previous section. You can't use ISBN numbers that are provided by KDP or other platforms.

The PCN program is intended for book publishers and not individual authors. However, all you need to do to be a publisher is to define an imprint name, maintain an office in the United States and be able answer questions about your books from that office.

To create an account, use the link below

https://www.loc.gov/publish/pcn/

And click on the link titled "Open an Account", read each of the sections that are linked from this page, then click on "Application to Participate" and fill out the form.

Once you've been accepted into the program, which occurs quickly, each time you want to publish a book, click the link below at least a week in advance of your publication date and fill in the information.

Once you've entered all the information into the form, it will be submitted, and generally anywhere from a day to a week you'll receive back your Library of Congress number. This needs to be recorded in several places.

- On the copyright page of your book.
- In the *Library of Congress Control Number* field of the ISBN database entry for your book on Bowker.com. This is on the first page of the listing.
- Entered with the book information when you define the book on Amazon, Draft2Digital, or other platform.

Keywords

Before you create your title, subtitle, description, or any other metadata, stop and come up with your keywords. Once you have those keywords defined, sprinkle them through your description, title, and subtitle.

Come up with a string of keywords that is about 400 characters long, each separated by a space. These don't need to be in any order. Don't include common words (stop words) such as "to", "the", "and" and so forth, and don't worry about plurals.

The way Amazon's keyword system works is simpler than most people think. KDP gives you seven keyword fields, and you can treat each one as a search phrase up to 50 characters long. Every word you enter becomes searchable independently. Amazon doesn't require you to enter phrases in any particular order, and it ignores common stop words like "the", "and", and "to". Don't repeat words from your title or subtitle in the keyword fields — Amazon already indexes those automatically, so duplicating them wastes space.

Think of keywords as describing what a reader would type into Amazon to find your book if they didn't know your title. They might search for a problem they're trying to solve, a topic they're curious about, a type of story they enjoy, or a specific situation they're in. Your job is to anticipate those searches and include the words that match them. Genre, setting, comparable authors, and reader situations are all fair game.

For example, let's say your book is about the history of television. You could come up with a string of words about the subjects you discuss in your book.

television American culture biography production handbook history platinum age criticism writing radio announcing TV antenna advertising actor actress

Your book can be discovered through searches on any of the keywords listed above. Enter this string of words into the keyword field in KDP. Note the newer version of KDP includes seven fields, so just split this up among them.

You can use the Bing Keyword Research Tool [19] to come up with words to use as keywords.

https://www.bing.com/webmasters/help/keyword-research-628070b6

You'll need to create a Microsoft account to use this tool, which is used to find keywords to purchase for Bing advertisements. However, you can use it just to find keywords without purchasing anything.

Sprinkle your keywords—and phrases—in your title, subtitle and description. Put your most important words and phrases near the front of these three fields.

---

[19] The Google Keyword Planner is no longer as useful as it was in the past because the results that are returned are generalized unless you've purchased Google ads.

Exercise–Practice using the Bing Keyword Research Tool to find keywords for your book or topic.

TITLE

A well-designed title can make the difference between a book that earns money and a book that sells poorly.

There are two audiences for your book title.

- People who might want to purchase your book.
- The indexing system of Amazon or your publishing company (and other search engines such as Google and Bing).

Your title and, to a lesser extent, the subtitle, should consider both audiences.

The title must be understandable by human beings and often needs to appeal to some emotion such as fear, anger, joy, greed, love or even hate. A good title is memorable, stands out from the competition, and communicates the subject of the fiction or nonfiction contents.

Amazon and search engines are looking for keywords and phrases to aid in indexing that book, so that people may find it when they're searching for information on a topic.

There are entire books and courses that teach how to create a good title, and there are many tools available that will construct a title out of keywords and phrases.

Some restrictions on a title are:

- As discussed in the section *Using Trademarks in the Title*, ensure you understand the legalities of using a trademark in the title of your book before you publish it.
- It is tempting to create a long, keywords stuffed title, and it is best to avoid this temptation. Keep it between 30 and 80 characters. You want long enough to communicate the meaning but not so long that it appears to be spammy.
- Your title must appear exactly as written on the cover image of your book. Amazon, and probably other platforms as well, reviews your title and cover at the point at which you publish to ensure this is true.
- You can change the title of a Kindle eBook any time you want, before and after you publish[20]. However, on a paperback, Amazon does not allow the title to be changed after the book has been published and made live. The titles of hardcover versions may not be changed either.

Amazon prioritizes keywords and phrases within the title higher than anything else in your book description, subtitle, keywords, and elsewhere. In addition, **keywords and phrases that are closer to the front of the title are given**

---

[20] Bowker states that once you've published a book with an ISBN number, the title, subtitle, author, series and so forth should not be changed, even for eBooks. However, the website will allow you to make changes, but the best practice is not to change your title and other metadata after publication.

priority over those near the end. For example, the words "make money" in the title "Make Money on Internet" are given more weight than in "Insider Tips on How to Make Money on the Internet".

Don't include advertising and promotions as part of your title (or subtitle)–for example, "free" or "reduced price". Don't reference other titles or authors, use the word best-selling or any other ranking, and only use a trademarked word when you have permission.

A well-written title with good keywords and phrases will get you more potential buyers than a poorly written title simply because of the way Amazon, and other search engines as well, creates its index.

SUBTITLE

The subtitle should communicate additional information about the content of your book. As with the title, avoid keyword stuffing and create a subtitle that is valuable to people and to Amazon and search engine indexing.

The keywords and key phrases within the subtitle don't carry as much weight as the title, but they are still used by Amazon to index the book.

According to Amazon's help page, the book title plus the subtitle together must be less than two hundred characters long.

Consider creating a book series. By doing this, you tell your readers that you'll be coming out with additional titles on that subject, and you can build promotional campaigns around that fact.

That's why in fiction you will commonly see trilogies or even longer series of books. Fans of those books get interested in the storyline and characters and want to read more. Authors who are on the ball and want to make more income can take advantage of this and create a series in the same universe as the first book.

This also works well for nonfiction in that you can create a series of books about business, home repair, finance, or many other topics. This allows you to create books that tie together and work to sell each other.

DESCRIPTION

It's a shame to spend money and effort to get people to your Amazon Book Page, only to turn them away with a poorly written book description.

Next to the cover and title, your book description is your most important selling tool. You have 4,000 characters, which is several pages, to entice lookers into buyers.

Your first sentence is the most important. Use it to grab your reader and pull them into the rest of the description. Start off with a shocking statement or question.

In the first few paragraphs, cater to emotions–anger, fear, hate, terror, love and joy are much more powerful than facts and reasoning. For non-fiction, show you understand their plight and are sympathetic–in fact, the book has the answers. For fiction, hint at a dark secret or a terror or something to that effect.

Once you've got the emotions stirred up, tell them a bit about what's in your book. Then go right back and stir up some emotions.

For nonfiction, include a bulleted list of some things they will learn. This helps with keywords (Amazon will use those in its search index) and informs your reader. Put this list near the bottom of your description–the emotions are more important.

Use HTML tags to format your description. The more useful ones are described below.

- <b> means to bold the text: <b>This is bolded</b>
-
 means insert a line break: Here's a line

- <h1> define a header: <h1>Header goes here</h1>
- <h2> to <h6> work the same as H1
- <hr> inserts a horizontal line: <hr>
- <i> is italics: <i>italicize this</i>
- <li> identifies a line in a bulleted or numbered list (see examples below)
- <p> defines a paragraph: <p>text goes here</p>
- <u> formats as underlined: <u>underline this</u>

An example of a bulleted list:

```
<ul>

        <li>Line 1</li>

        <li>Line 2</li>

</ul>
```

And a numbered list:

```
<ol>

        <li>List 1</li>

        <li>List 2</li>

</ol>
```

Use HTML to format your description so that it stands out from all the others on Amazon. Use <h1> for your primary headings, create a bulleted list for your benefits and such, and use <b> and <i> to emphasize keywords and important points.

An important distinction: your book description is indexed by Google as well as Amazon. Amazon indexes keywords from your keyword fields and title. Google indexes your description as web content. Keyword stuffing your description — cramming in repeated phrases — can hurt your Google indexing without helping your Amazon ranking. Write your description for readers first. Discoverability comes from good writing, not tricks that search engines are built to penalize.

My early book descriptions were terrible, and I didn't know it. I had been trained on affiliate marketing copy — long-form sales pages with multiple headlines, benefit stacks, and calls to action stacked on top of each other. That style works for selling courses and supplements. For books on Amazon, it looks like spam. I was writing descriptions that ran the full 4,000 characters, formatted like a sales page, and readers could smell the desperation. Sales were flat.

Writing a good book description is a copywriting skill — and copywriting is something most authors haven't been trained in. I hadn't either, not for books. It took real time and failure to understand the difference between a description that informs and one that converts. AI makes drafting easier now, but the output tends to be flat and generic — it hits the structure without the emotional specificity that makes someone click buy. Use it as a starting point and rewrite in your own voice. The before-and-after example below shows what the difference looks like in practice.

GOOD DESCRIPTION VS. BAD DESCRIPTION

Here's what a bad description looks like. It's the kind authors write when they're thinking about their book instead of their reader:

> *This book is about self-publishing. It covers writing, publishing, and marketing your books on Amazon and other platforms. The author has many years of experience and shares his knowledge in this comprehensive guide. Topics include book covers, metadata, social media, email lists, and more. Whether you are a beginner or have some experience, this book has something for everyone.*

Notice what's wrong. It leads with what the book is about instead of what the reader's problem is. "This book is about..." is the weakest possible opening. It tells you nothing about whether this book is for you specifically. "Has something for everyone" means it's for no one in particular. And "journey" is doing no work. The reader clicks away.

Here's a better version of the same book, using the structure described above:

You wrote the book. So why isn't it selling?

Most self-published authors sell fewer than a dozen copies — almost all to people they know. Not because the book is bad. Because nobody found it, nobody trusted it, and nobody clicked buy. That's a business problem, not a writing problem.

Richard Lowe left a six-figure corporate career at 53 to become a full-time self-published author and ghostwriter. In three years he published and ghostwrote over 113 books. This is the book he wished existed when he started — a ground-level, no-scam guide to building a real income from self-publishing.

Inside you'll learn:

• How to research a topic before you write a single word — so you don't spend six months on a book nobody wants

• The metadata, cover, and description decisions that determine whether Amazon shows your book to anyone

• How to build a platform that actually sells books — without spending your writing time on social media

• Why quantity matters more than you think, and how to publish fast without publishing badly

• The scams, schemes, and expensive courses that will drain your bank account without moving your career forward

If you're serious about making a living from your writing — not just publishing a book and hoping — this is the guide that tells you how it actually works.

The difference between the two examples is clear. The bad one describes a book. The good one talks to a person with a specific problem. It opens with the reader's frustration, not the author's credentials. It leads with a question that stings a little if you're in that situation. The credentials come in paragraph two, but only after the reader already feels understood. The bullet points are written as outcomes, not topics — notice they each end with a reason the reader cares, not just a subject heading. And the closing doesn't say "buy this book" — it says this is for people who are serious, which is more compelling because it implies not everyone qualifies.

Use your own book as practice. Write the bad version first — just describe what's in it. Then rewrite it starting with the reader's problem. You'll see the difference immediately.

CATEGORIES

Imagine a bookstore or library with books randomly placed on shelves anywhere in the establishment with no order. Would this make it difficult to find the books that you want?

KDP uses an industry-standard system called BISAC codes, which categorize books into various subjects. One way to think of it is that these codes define the bookshelves for your books.

Amazon uses these codes as a base and translates them into its own structure of organization. This can make it confusing to find the right code for your book, since the category that you found on Amazon may not match a BISAC code.

For your books on KDP, you can choose two codes.

A good way to determine the categories is to look at those used by similar books.

Some sample categories from one of my coloring books are shown below.

Books > Arts & Photography > Drawing > Coloring Books for Grown-Ups

Books > Crafts, Hobbies & Home > Crafts & Hobbies

You'll find many books that have over two categories, and you'll find other books that are in categories that don't exist in the BISAC structure.

Categories matter more than most authors realize. They determine which bestseller lists your book appears on, which browse pages Amazon shows it on, and which "customers also bought" chains your book gets pulled into. A book in the wrong category is invisible. A book in a well-chosen, slightly less competitive category can hit a bestseller ranking within days of launch and display that orange bestseller banner on its page indefinitely — which drives more clicks.

KDP lets you choose two categories at publication, but you can get up to ten by contacting Amazon support directly after your book is live. This is one of the most underused moves in self-publishing. Email KDP and ask them to add specific additional categories by name. Give them the exact category path — for example, "Books > Business & Money > Skills > Time Management" — and they will usually add them within a few days. Do this for every book.

To find the right categories, start by searching Amazon for your topic and opening the pages of three to five books that are directly comparable to yours. Scroll to the Product Details section and look at their current rankings by category, with the full path shown. Note every category your competitors are in. Then check which ones have the lowest-ranked books at the top — those are the less competitive categories where a new book can crack the top ten more easily.

Some categories that appear on Amazon don't exist in the KDP dropdown at all — they can only be added by customer service. This is why it's worth browsing your topic on Amazon directly rather than relying only on what KDP shows you during setup. If you see a category that fits your book and competitors are ranking in it, request it. Amazon will usually oblige.

One more thing: avoid categories that are wildly off-topic just because they're low competition. Amazon's algorithm notices when readers in a category don't engage with your book, and that hurts your ranking across the board. Stay relevant. The goal is to be the right book in a thinner crowd, not a misplaced book in an empty room.

Two tools I use regularly for category research are KDSpy and KDRocket. KDSpy is a browser extension that pulls sales rank, estimated sales, reviews, and category data directly from Amazon pages — making it much faster to scan and compare categories across multiple books. KDRocket is a standalone desktop tool that helps you find high-opportunity categories and keywords by showing you competition levels and estimated sales volumes. Between the two, you can cut hours of manual Amazon browsing down to minutes. Neither is free, but for anyone publishing more than a handful of books, they pay for themselves quickly.

Exercise—Search Amazon for a book similar to one you're planning to write. Open three or four of the top results and note every category listed in their Product Details. Which categories have the lowest bestseller rank numbers at their top spot? Those are your targets. Request them from KDP support after you publish.

One thing most authors miss: categories are not permanent. You can change them any time by contacting KDP support, and you should revisit them regularly. If a category is not producing results, try a different one. Ranking well in one category generates real sales, and those sales signal to Amazon that your book is performing — which helps your visibility in harder, more competitive categories as well.

The strategy: find a category that is active — real books selling in it — but not dominated by mega-bestsellers. Rank well there and it lifts your visibility in the harder categories you actually want. KDSpy is excellent for identifying these opportunities. Look for categories where the top books have moderate sales ranks rather than titles with thousands of reviews.

CONCLUSIONS

Spend the time creating the metadata for your book. This information is used by Amazon to create your Book Page, to help readers find your books, and as submissions to search engines and book indexes.

Decisions about your title, subtitle, series name, and ISBN can dramatically affect your sales. A poorly thought-out title, for example, can make your book unfindable or unattractive to your readers.

Chapter 12: Parts of a Book

When I started, I was obsessive about this. Library of Congress numbers for everything. Researched the perfect copyright page format. Made sure every element of front and back matter was exactly right according to the standards. My books were technically flawless in that department.

I\'ve since relaxed considerably. Readers don\'t care. Libraries care a little, booksellers care slightly, and nobody else cares at all. I now use a simple copyright page on every book and don\'t stress about the rest. The standards in this chapter are worth knowing so you understand what each element is for — but don\'t let perfecting your front matter become a reason to delay publishing. A technically impeccable book that sits in a folder is worth nothing. Get it out.

One caveat: if you're pursuing hybrid or traditional publishing, the publisher will handle this for you and will have their own standards. This chapter is for self-publishers. Know the elements, use them correctly, and don't obsess.

Note: Divide your book into these parts for publishing on KDP or Lulu. Draft2Digital can, optionally, insert many of these for you.

The standards for eBooks differ slightly from those for paperbacks and hardcovers. This puts more of the actual book at the front of eBooks where it can be seen in the "look inside" feature available on Amazon and other publishers. Platforms such as Amazon take the first 10% or so of your book and make it available on the Book Page so that readers can review a chapter or two to get an idea of what the book is about before they make a purchase.

If you fill up the *look inside* preview with copyright, series, and other materials, readers cannot preview what your book is about, and you are less likely to make a sale.

Because of this, it is acceptable either to move some of the front material to the back (such as a list of an author's other books, traditionally part of the front material) or skip including it entirely.

The title page and copyright page should always be at the front of eBooks.

Paperbacks and hardcovers are typically printed on the front and back of each page. The preface, introduction, table of contents, and each chapter should begin on an odd-numbered page, and some other information such as the copyright and series pages begin on in even page.

FRONT MATTER

At the front, there are typically several pages set aside that identify the contents, subject and other information about the book.

ENDORSEMENTS PAGE

If you get endorsements for your book before publication, you can include them on a page in front of everything. Endorsements are especially valuable from known influencers and leaders in your target audience. This is always on the odd page, and the back (even page) should be blank.

An endorsement page is optional in the eBook version.

HALF TITLE PAGE

The half-title page contains only your book title and author name, centered and in a large font, placed about a third of the way down the page. You can also include the subtitle, although this is not standard. This page is typically not included in eBooks.

FRONTISPIECE

This is an illustration on the back of the half-title page. For coloring, puzzle and comic books, include one drawing from inside the book so it will show up in the "Look Inside" feature on the Amazon book page.

You can include either a frontispiece or a series page but not both.

This is typically not included in eBooks.

As a note, on my coloring books, I include a sample or two on the Frontispiece so that it shows up on the "Look Inside" for the book.

THE SERIES PAGE OR OTHER BOOKS PAGE

This section appears on the back of the half-title page and contains a list of previously published books. Some authors list them from most recent to oldest, and others list them by series. This is not included in eBooks.

If you want to include a list of your other titles and series in an eBook, add it to the *back matter* instead of the *front matter*.

THE TITLE PAGE

The title page is always on the odd side, and includes the book title, subtitle, author, and publisher name.

THE COPYRIGHT PAGE

See the chapter on publishing for information about the copyright page.

DEDICATION

Optionally, a few words or sentences dedicating the book to someone or an organization. This takes up a full odd-numbered page. The back page should be blank.

FOREWORD

An introduction is a short essay, usually written by someone else, to help promote or introduce the book. It begins on an odd page, and the numbering is typically in lower-case Roman numerals beginning with "i".

PREFACE

This is the introduction written by the author to explain how the book came about. You can include a personal anecdote or story to give the reader some context for the book. It begins on an odd page number.

ACKNOWLEDGEMENTS

Write as much as you want to acknowledge anyone who helped you create the book. Some authors get very specific and thank everyone who even remotely helped; others just thank a few friends; and many leave this section off entirely. This begins on an odd page.

The table of contents can be automatically generated based upon header styles by Microsoft Word and other word processers. In Word, these are Heading 1, Heading 2 and so on. If you use the built-in styles for headings, you can generate your table of contents automatically.

For paperbacks and hardcovers, the page numbers are included in the table of contents. For eBooks, page numbers are not included. Instead, each link in the table of contents should be a clickable link to the page in the book.

Important note: Sometimes you'll find tables of contents placed at the end of the book in eBooks. Amazon frowns upon this practice and prefers this to be placed at the front.

LIST OF ILLUSTRATIONS

Optionally, list any illustrations or photos included in your book.

LIST OF TABLES

Optionally, list any tables included in the book.

INTRODUCTION

The introduction serves to summarize or present the subject of the book. This can be as short or as long as you want and begins on an odd page.

There are a lot of sections that you could put at the back of the book. Traditionally, nonfiction books include an index, an author biography (about the author), a list of references if applicable, and possibly a glossary if there are technical terms.

However, there is no reason you can't include more (or even less). In the modern world of self-publishing, whether digital or print on demand, there is little concern about space or the cost of these extra pages[21]. Don't go overboard but include extra materials if you see fit.

Take advantage of the space to give your reader more information, to tell them about yourself, help them find things in the book or give them definitions, and advertise your other books and services.

REFERENCES

For nonfiction works, include a list of any books or other materials that you believe will help your readers. This is an optional section.

GLOSSARY

Optionally, include a list of words and definitions to help your readers when they run into technical or obscure language. Note: you cannot just copy definitions from the

---

[21] There is a cost-per-page for paperbacks; the more pages in the book, the higher the price you will need to charge. For Kindle, you are charged to send the book to the Kindle, but unless you have a lot of large images, this cost is very low.

dictionary–that's copyright infringement. Paraphrase the definitions in your own words.

END NOTES

If you have any citations in your nonfiction book, list them here.

Citing your sources is good form. Not doing so is plagiarism. Always cite your sources.

INDEX

Most eBooks don't include indexes since the contents can be searched directly from Kindle or other eBook readers. However, if that book also appears in paperback or hardcover, then you might include an index in those editions.

Creating an index is not as easy as you would think. It's not just a matter of finding every occurrence of certain words or keywords, marking them in your word processor, and listing them in a table at the back of the book. This creates a relatively useless hodgepodge of chaos that is difficult to use and doesn't serve the purpose of an index.

The reason an index exists is to give your readers the ability to find the important passages related to a specific keyword or phrase directly, without having to read the rest of the book.

Definitions or vital information may be bolded in the index, and titles of books may be italicized. You can also specify a page number or range of page numbers.

Thus, you don't want to mark every single occurrence of a keyword. Instead, pick out the references that are important to your readers; the ones that give them an

241

answer to whatever question is on their mind at that point in time.

Short nonfiction paperback or hardbound books don't require indexes. However, in a longer work, you might create one.

Your word processor should include the ability to mark entries for the index and then use that to create the actual index itself. For example, the indexing capabilities of Microsoft Word are excellent and easy to use.

If you decide to create an index for your book, be sure to do it right. Read through some resources listed on asindexing.org before you start or, if you have the budget, hire someone to do it for you.

ABOUT THE AUTHOR

You should always include an *About the Author* section in the back of your book. This can be as short or long as you want, but one to three pages is more than enough.

The purpose of this is to present a biography of yourself, or, with a pen name, of a made-up person. This is your opportunity to build your brand and add to your credibility.

This section is written in the third person as if someone were talking about you. However, sometimes first-person works just fine, especially if a little bit of humor is injected.

This is a great place for you to talk about your life as an author, why you started writing, your background, and anything else that you feel would interest your readers.

Always include a picture, a headshot, to give your readers an idea of who you are. Of course, if you're writing under a pen name, that may be more difficult. Some authors may use a drawing, and others may skip the picture entirely.

I recommend you include a link to your website, LinkedIn and Facebook profiles (if you have them), and your X name. If you want to be contacted via email, please also include your email address.

Remember this is not a sales page, and you should not use this opportunity to sell products or services or other books that you have written.

Chapter 13: The Copyright Page

Don't overthink this. There are plenty of good copyright page templates online — find one that fits your book type, use it, and move on. The copyright page exists to protect you legally, and a standard template does that job fine.

What does matter: disclaimers. If your book contains any kind of advice — medical, legal, financial, fitness, or otherwise — include a disclaimer making clear you are not a licensed professional and readers should consult one before acting on anything you've written. Put it in its own clearly labeled section, not buried in small print. A prominent disclaimer reduces your legal exposure significantly. Same goes for fiction that could be read as referring to real people or events.

COPYRIGHT NOTICE

All copyright pages require the copyright notice. This short line defines exactly who owns the copyright of the book.

- Begin with a copyright symbol ©, the word "Copyright" or both. Using (c) should be avoided as it may not stand up in court.
- The year the work was published for the first time.
- The name of the copyright owner, which can be a pen name.

Note that your work is copyrighted (at least in the United States) from the moment it was created, and you do not need to file with the copyright office. However, registering your work with the copyright office is valuable if you need to prove in court that you have the rights to the work.

Rights

Next, include a paragraph describing the rights you allow and disallow for your work. Typically, this includes the words "All rights reserved" followed by a few sentences describing how the work may or may not be used.

The rest of the legalese depends on your requirements and what protections you believe you need.

If you use any trademarks within your book that don't belong to you, it's wise to include a paragraph stating that you're using them in editorial fashion and don't intend to infringe.

Depending on your needs, the legalese can be much longer or shorter.

If you went to the trouble of getting an LOCC number, then include that on your copyright page.

ISBN

Include the ISBN number of your book, if you have one. If you have multiple versions, such as an eBook, paperback and hardcover, list the ISBN numbers of each edition.

I like to include the ASIN number of the eBook version, which identifies it in the Amazon database. Note if you include the ASIN number, you will need to publish the eBook, get the ASIN number that was assigned upon publication, insert it into your copyright page, and then republish the eBook with the updated information.

Do not include words such as Amazon, Kindle, or the equivalent from other publishers. If you ever want to publish your book on platforms such as Apple Books, which is the Apple bookstore, your book will be rejected if you include competitor names on the copyright page or elsewhere in the text.

Thus, if you have an ISBN for the Barnes & Noble Nook tablet and an ISBN for your Kindle version, simply list them both as eBooks without specifying the tablet type.

Contributors

It is good to include a list of those who contributed to the book in the last section of your copyright page. This includes book designers, proofreaders, editors, cover designers, indexers, and anyone else that helped you with any part of your book.

Conclusions

Once you've defined one copyright page, you can use it as a template for all your other books.

The copyright page is vital, as it communicates the legalities associated with your book. It contains other information in a standard location that is available to libraries, bookstores and indexes.

Chapter 14: Publishing

My first time publishing on KDP was rough. The interface was nothing like what it is now, and Amazon hadn't yet sorted out the mess from acquiring CreateSpace. For a while you had two separate systems that didn't talk to each other properly, and KDP itself was touchy — small formatting errors would kick your file back, and the error messages were not helpful. It took several attempts to get each book through. Once Amazon fixed the interface and merged everything into one dashboard, it got dramatically better. But the early days were a genuine slog.

I also tried Smashwords early on. It was a disaster. Their formatting requirements were extraordinarily specific — they called it the "Smashwords Style Guide" and it was dozens of pages of rules about how your Word document had to be set up before they would accept it. I spent countless hours trying to meet their specifications and kept getting rejected. Eventually I gave up, deleted everything, and moved on. Smashwords no longer operates as it did — it merged with Draft2Digital in 2022 — and D2D's process is dramatically simpler. Don't let old horror stories about Smashwords put you off wide distribution. The current tools are nothing like that.

Publishing is much easier now than it was when I started. What was genuinely difficult has been smoothed out. What remains is just a learning curve — terminology, formatting requirements, and knowing which options matter and which you can ignore. Go through it slowly the first time, read the help files, and expect to make a few mistakes. By the third or fourth book it becomes routine.

Before diving into how publishing works, it's worth making the case for why self-publishing is often the right choice. A successful self-published author I interviewed laid it out clearly. Creative control is the first thing: as a self-publisher, you are your own publishing director. You have total say in the title, cover design, presentation, and how it's sold. A trade-published author typically has very little say in any of that.

Speed is the second factor. If you signed a contract with a major publisher today, the book probably wouldn't appear until late next year. Self-publishing moves on your schedule — months, not years.

The financial factor is significant. A trade-published author typically receives 5 to 10 percent of the cover price. Self-publishing an ebook in the popular price ranges on Amazon gets you 70 percent. The math is not subtle.

The marketing myth is the fourth point, and probably the most important one for authors considering traditional publishing as an escape from having to promote themselves. Unless you are already a celebrity or an established bestseller, a trade publisher will not spend meaningful time on your book's marketing. You might get a day or a day and a half of a publicist's time. The marketing still largely falls to you — except now you have less money and less control to do it with.

Another author I interviewed put his reasons plainly: he hates writing query letters, and he wants creative control. He's never been a conformist — self-publishing suited his personality before it suited his business model. Those are valid reasons too. The traditional publishing path requires patience, tolerance for rejection, and willingness to give up significant control over the finished product. Self-publishing requires none of that. It requires different things — discipline, marketing, and business sense — but the gatekeepers are gone.

Focus on Amazon

In this book, we are primarily concerned with publishing on Amazon because it's by far the largest market for self-published books.

One of the great things about self-publishing is that you have a lot more options than you do if you go with a traditional publisher. You get to choose things such as the price of the book, its dimensions (width and height), whether it's black-and-white or color, and even more importantly, its format (eBook, paperback, hardcover, and so on).

Although your sales opportunities are by far the greatest with Amazon, there are several other publishers that you can choose for your book. These include Lulu, IngramSpark, Apple Books, Kobo and Barnes & Noble, to name a few. Each of these has its advantages and disadvantages, and some of them can sell their books through Amazon.

KDP Select

When you publish your book on Kindle using KDP, you have the option of placing your book into KDP Select. This gives you additional royalty and promotional opportunities.

Currently, the benefits include:

- If an Amazon customer joins Kindle Unlimited, they can read Kindle eBooks free. If you opt into KDP Select, your book can be read for free, and you receive a share of the KDP Select Global Fund.
- You earn 70% royalties for sales in Japan, India, Brazil and Mexico.
- Every 90 days, you can use either a countdown deal or a free promotion for about a week. The countdown deal shows a countdown clock next to the price.

On the downside, by opting into KDP Select, your book may not be electronically distributed in any other format at any price, including free. This means you cannot sell an electronic version from your blog, website, or other eBook formats.

Should you enroll your books in Kindle Select? The benefits are substantial—I've seen a definite increase in my income because of the program.

One reason NOT to include your book in the program is if you want to sell it on a platform such as Draft2Digital, Apple Books, or even directly download from your blog.

FORMATS

If you decide you want to stick with Amazon as your book publisher, you have three options: Kindle, paperback and audiobook. Considering that you can publish to each for no cost, you'd be wise to publish your books on all three. Of course, coloring books, puzzle books, and other consumables can't be published as audiobooks or on the Kindle.

Paperback

Paperbacks are published using KDP.COM. These are actual physical books, which are printed on demand. This means that they are created immediately after a customer orders. There is no upfront charge for using KDP–but you'll split the profits with them if the book sells.

Kindle

Kindle is an electronic book format that works on Amazon's proprietary Kindle eReaders (they also provide applications for most other devices). Books published in this format cannot include niceties such as numbered lists, positioned graphics, and many other things that you can use in paperbacks to make your books more attractive. These electronic books are published using kdp.com.

I've written a book that goes into detail about self-publishing on Kindle called *How to Publish on Kindle*. This book goes through each step of the process from beginning to end.

Audiobook

Audiobooks are recordings of your book. You can choose to record these yourself or use acx.com (owned by Amazon) to hire someone to do it for you. Here, you have the option of choosing a royalty split with the actor or paying them directly and taking 100% of the royalties.

If you want to publish a hardcover version of your book, then you must use the services of Ingramspark.com or Lulu.com. I went to the trouble of creating hardcover copies of all my nonfiction books and was surprised that they sell relatively well. I took advantage of a coupon from IngramSpark so the publishing was free. Both Lulu and IngramSpark sell books through Amazon and other distributors.

WHICH FORMAT?

For every non-consumable book you publish, create at a minimum a Kindle eBook, a paperback and an audiobook version. Each of these appeals to a different audience, and you find that you'll receive sales spread over all three types of books.

Not publishing books in all three formats is leaving money on the table. Since there is no cost involved in creating any of them, except for time, I recommend you go through the trouble to do it.

You can also create a hardcover on IngramSpark which will be sold on Amazon. Ingram charges a small fee–take advantage of their regularly released coupons.

RETURNS

When you publish paperbacks or hardcovers on IngramSpark, never allow returns. Before you publish, make sure the option to allow returns is set to NO, and double-check it again.

This is important because if set to YES, bookstores have the option to return books that don't sell. IngramSpark will refund that money to them from your account balance, and you'll get mailed the books, which are often in terrible, unusable condition.

If you accidentally set this option to YES then change it to NO, returns will be allowed for 6 months.

In theory, allowing returns makes it more likely that bookstores will purchase your books, since they don't have the risk associated with not selling. As a small publisher, you shouldn't take that risk yourself.

Save yourself the time and hassle by not allowing returns.

OTHER ELECTRONIC FORMATS

Besides Kindle, there are several other electronic formats to choose from. However, eBooks enrolled in KDP Select can't be published in any of these other formats because of the terms and conditions of that program.

If your book is not enrolled in KDP Select, two good choices for publishing are the Apple Books and the Nook. Apple Books is Apple's platform for electronic books, and the Nook is supported by Barnes & Noble.

You can also publish your book in PDF format. PDF stands for Portable Document Format, and it was created by Adobe to allow documents to be viewed on any platform, including Windows, Apple, Linux, tablets and elsewhere.

PDF is valuable for creating a version of your book that is downloadable from your blog or elsewhere. I commonly use it to give away the first or second chapter of a book for free as a teaser. Microsoft Word has a "save to PDF" option, or you can use many PDF conversion tools available on the web.

DRAFT2DIGITAL

You can manually submit your book in the proper format to all the various publishers, and there are quite a few of them, or you could use one of the publishing aggregators such as Draft2Digital.

This company accepts your document in Word or PDF format, validates it, converts it, and sends it off to each publisher (excluding Amazon) for you. They pay you royalties based upon sales and have a reporting system seeking to keep track of how things are doing.

If you don't have an Apple computer system, using an aggregator such as this is the easiest way to get your book published in Apple Book's format. Otherwise, you'll have to get access to an Apple system, because the software doesn't run on Windows.

CONCLUSIONS

First, publishing can seem like a confusing process. There are many options and words unique to the publishing industry, and the learning curve can be steep.

Take your time, read the tutorials and help files for each format, and you'll get through it just fine. Once you've published a few books, the entire process becomes second nature.

Chapter 15: Networking

One of the most important things that you can do to advance your writing career is to build a network of other writers, publishers, promoters, and readers. This was one of the most difficult things for me, since I am introverted and prefer writing in front of a keyboard over being in a group of people at an event.

Regardless, it is vital that all self-published authors find people in their area and on the Internet who can both help them and whom they can help.

Networking works both ways–in fact, the best way to network is to give without receiving a benefit. This is easier than it sounds.

For example, I have many contacts with outsourcers who can help with proofreading, book covers, promotion, formatting and so forth. If someone in my network approaches me for help in creating a book cover, I can refer them to one of several book cover creators.

The idea is to help people, and that help doesn't need to come from themselves. Once you become known as someone who has the contacts for anything, you'll be amazed at how quickly a group forms around you.

You can network just about anywhere. In your local area, check out local writing groups, associations, libraries, and even networking groups or your Chamber of Commerce. On the Internet, join writing groups on Facebook, LinkedIn, and other social media and search out and join writing associations.

It is very difficult to make a living in a vacuum. As with any profession, you need help from other people. Sure, you can write that book all by yourself with no help from anyone–but there are only so many hours in the day and doing all the things that you need to do to be successful as a professional writer may take more time than you have.

You have the option of outsourcing, which means paying other people to do work for you. It's relatively easy to find people on the web who will do high-quality jobs for you at inexpensive prices. After all, you have the entire planet to choose from.

Outsourcing requires money, and it can add up quickly, especially if you publish more than one book.

Remember, you need to have your book proofread and edited; you need to create a cover–or more likely, more than one; you need to write an enticing book description for Amazon or wherever you're selling your book; you'll need to promote and market your manuscript; if you're doing book signings and speeches, then you may need to pay for travel expenses.

As you can see, the cost can add up quickly if you want to produce a good quality book and you want it to sell.

To help you in your efforts to become a professional writer who's making a living, you need to build a network and engage your audience.

The best way to build a network is to find other writers and form relationships with them. Join writing groups on social media sites such as LinkedIn, Facebook, Instagram, and so forth, and begin having conversations with writers, and eventually you'll find a few who will work with you in a partnership of sorts.

Don't forget about real-world places to meet writers such as bookstores, libraries, writing associations, your local Chamber of Commerce, networking groups, and meetup groups. These organizations (and many more) are useful for finding kindred spirits who will exchange services.

For example, within a network of writers, you can exchange books to proofread. You send them a copy of your book, perhaps chapter by chapter, to proofread, and they do the same and send their books to you.

If you can connect with some people who are skilled at graphics, you might offer to write or change their website copy for art on a book cover.

Work your network for referrals as well. If you need to create a book cover, put the word out to your writing network, and more than likely you'll soon find yourself hooked up with a good book cover artist.

One key to making this work is that you need to be willing to give and to receive. When another writer asks you for a referral, you need to give it to them.

To keep your group engaged, I have found the best thing to do is to create a Facebook group. Post frequently, at least once a day; otherwise, the group may become inactive. Stir the pot occasionally or find a couple of motivated members who will do it for you.

You might be tempted to use your team to help you get reviews about your books but avoid that temptation. Amazon's terms and conditions about book reviews explicitly don't allow friends or business associates to review each other's books. Creating a group to trade book reviews clearly violates the terms and conditions and could get your Amazon account suspended or even deleted.

However, nothing prevents you from getting reviews or testimonials from your team for other purposes. For example, you might ask a team member to write a book review for your website or to include in your promotional copy.

Just be careful that you thoroughly understand the terms and conditions of any place you post reviews of this nature. Obviously, if you put them on your own blog or in your own promotional materials, there won't be a problem.

For a one-to-one exchange, such as, "I'll proofread chapter 4 of your book if you proofread chapter 12 of mine", an oral agreement is just fine. After all, there's not much to lose.

However, I've learned through hard experience that for more complicated or long-lasting exchanges, a written agreement is best. This agreement, while it doesn't have to be a legal document, should spell out what's expected of both parties, timing, and so forth.

For example, if you create an exchange with another writer to write an article for their blog every other week for proofreading, write up a memo stating who does what, under what conditions, and for how long. Otherwise, the exchange becomes muddy, and hard feelings probably result.

Building a team of fellow writers and other creative people is a great way to use the power of many to help you succeed as a professional writer. It gives you over twenty-four hours in a day because you are using hours from other people's days.

Take Part in Writing Associations

One of the best ways to network is to take part in writing associations. There are associations at a local level, often working with libraries, for entire states, regions, and even nationally. Most, if not all, of them have Internet sites to allow you to network online.

A few of them that I've found are useful are listed below.

The Alliance of Independent Authors

This organization operates throughout the world and is dedicated to helping self-publishing writers and authors who provide services.

Nonfiction Authors Association

The Nonfiction Authors Association provides services to nonfiction authors by putting on tele seminars, posting articles and providing services.

Authors Guild

The Author's Guild provides support for authors and maintains a community where you can find help if you need it.

Spend the time to create quality business cards. By this I mean hiring a graphics artist or designer to work with you to create a business card that projects your image precisely.

Sure, you can jump online to one of those online self-service companies and order a box of plain Jane, same as everybody else boring cards. In fact, when you're first starting out and you have a small budget, that's exactly the thing to do.

However, as soon as you have enough money in your budget, after you've secured your blog hosting and a few other things, spend the money and do it right.

Your business card needs to show you in the best possible light. It needs to have the correct colors and fonts, your logo, and the proper combination of these things to promote your self-publishing and author brands.

You can expect to spend a couple of hundred dollars or more getting your cards designed, although many times it is possible to trade your writing services for their design services.

Create business cards that you'll be proud to hand out to everyone, that you feel so good that they practically fly out of your hands.

Pass out your business cards wherever you go. They don't do any good sitting in a box in a drawer in your house or in the trunk of your car. Hand them out to everyone, but make sure you give each person a firm handshake, find out their name, and strike up a conversation with them, even if it only lasts for a few minutes. Give them a reason to keep your business card on the top of their pile rather than throwing it into a drawer where it rots for years unseen and unused.

One of the great things about having business cards is that it adds to the feeling that your company and your business is real. Having a card with your well-designed logo, your selection of fonts and colors, and your contact information is part of being in business and doing it well.

Besides, in the world of networking, there is little worse than being asked for a business card and having to make some lame excuse why you don't have one.

Oh yes, I know that these days many smartphones let people exchange contact information by tapping their screens together. As a computer security expert, that kind of interaction between my phone and your phone makes me shudder.

Business cards work much better because they are physical, tangible assets. You can hand them to people, shake their hands, and introduce yourself. It's hard to do that with a cell phone.

Conclusions

Build your network and help people without keeping score. The authors and collaborators you connect with will save you time, expand your reach, and occasionally save you from expensive mistakes. Nobody does this alone.

Chapter 16: Keep the Money Flowing

The next challenge that you'll face is building your writing and publishing "empire" up to where it is giving you a steady and respectable income. The difficulty is not creating a single book that sells well–with some hard work, a strong focus, some significant promotion, and a little bit of luck you can make it sell very well for a short time.

My first bestseller, *Focus on LinkedIn*, did exceptionally well. Because I had gotten many reviews and promoted heavily using a service (which no longer exists), I sold a thousand copies within a single day. Building on that success, I quickly submitted the book to BookBub, was accepted, and sold another five thousand copies.

Unfortunately, the book tanked after that, and I could not rebuild that success with that title. Sure, the book sells well when priced at ninety-nine cents and is blasted to a targeted email list comprising 440,000 addresses. However, when priced at a more respectable point, $4.99, sales dropped until the book sold just a few copies a week.

That experience is not unique among self-published authors. A friend of mine published a coloring book, which she promoted heavily at a highly reduced price. She sold over two thousand copies in a few days. However, when the book was priced to where she could make a decent royalty, sales dropped and never recovered.

Selling a few hundred or a few thousand copies of your title in a brief time feels very good and even priced at ninety-nine cents you make a good chunk of change.

But you can't run a business that way–spikes and valleys in your income make it hard to predict how much you're going to make from day to day, week to week and month to month. Unpredictable income makes it hard to pay predictable bills such as rent, credit cards, car payments and utilities.

Thus, your focus should be on creating a writing and publishing business that produces a stream of income that is predictable and relatively secure.

Two important points to consider are:

- One or two books can go up and down in sales rapidly and sometimes unpredictably.
- The more books you publish, the more this tendency will even out.

As I've stressed several times in this book, your focus should be on producing quality books as fast as possible.

There are opportunities for income from sources other than just the royalties from selling your book.

We'll go over some options that are available to help you produce a steady, relatively predictable stream of income from your self-publishing career.

Write as Many Books as Fast as You Can

Regardless of whether you write fiction or nonfiction, illustrate children's books, publish coloring or puzzle books, or produce comic books, to create a reliable income–the prerequisite for quitting your full-time job–you need to focus on quantity.

Quantity is more important than quality, and quality is more important than length.

What does that mean?

LENGTH

Let's begin with length. What is the ideal length for a book? If you're trying to make a living as a self-published author, it turns out that shorter is better–up to a point. Look at it this way; you can probably write, publish, promote and sell ten 10,000-word books in less time than it takes to write one 100,000-word book.

For example, suppose you spend six months writing 100,000-word novel, then you publish it and promote it to the world. For the entire six months, your novel has produced no income. When you publish the book, you'll probably price it at something like $9.95 for the Kindle version and $16.95 for the paperback, and you may sell a few hundred or even a thousand copies.

If you wrote eight 10,000-word books that each took three weeks to write, proofread, publish and promote, then you would begin making money, at least potentially, within three weeks of beginning that process.

You'd probably price one of these smaller books at $3.99 for the Kindle version and $6.95 for the paperback. At the much lower price point, with some moderate promotion, you'll probably sell anywhere from a few dozen to a few hundred copies a month.

Thus, if you sold 10 Kindle copies and 5 paperbacks of the 100,000-word novel, your gross sales would $184.25 and your royalties probably around $100.

On shorter books, if you sold the same number of each, gross profits would be $74.65 each, or $597.20 total for all of them.

In this simplified example, not only would you make over three times the income from the smaller books, but you'd begin earning money on the publication of the first one in the third week rather than after six months of writing.

This also means you have more chances of "getting it right." With only one novel after six months, you are taking a big gamble regarding the time that the book will sell well enough to justify that much work. If the book doesn't sell well, then you will have lost all that time with little to show for it.

With eight books, you have more chances to succeed. One of those eight might sell very well, 2 or 3 might sell okay, and the other 4 could bomb. But at least you have the potential to get income after the third week (in this example).

Kindle readers (at least) prefer shorter books; they favor quick reads that they can digest over lunch or in an evening than a long novel or non-fiction volume.

The point is to focus on creating books in the 10,000 to 15,000-word range.

QUALITY

Even though quantity is more important than quality in the world of self-publishing, that doesn't mean that you shouldn't spend the time and effort to ensure that your book is of high quality and presents good value to your readers.

A poor-quality book that is rife with misspellings and grammar errors, that is poorly organized and that doesn't provide value to your readers can sabotage your self-publishing career.

Take pride in your work, and make it show by producing the best books that you can produce.

Make sure you proofread your books for grammar and spelling errors. Modern word processors, at least if they are any good, include reasonable grammar and spelling checkers. Take advantage of them to catch a few errors.

Use a service such as grammarly.com and autocrit.com, among others, to further check your work for errors.

Before sending your book to anyone else to read, it's a good idea to read through the entire thing out loud twice, on separate days. I'm constantly amazed at how many errors I uncover by the simple fact of having read it out loud.

Hiring another person to proofread your book is a good idea, and you'll have to decide whether the benefit is worth the cost. There are many good proofreaders on Fiverr.com that will proofread your book for very good rates.

If you can't afford a proofreader, or if you don't expect to sell enough books to justify the cost, then see if you can exchange services (barter) with another writing friend and get them to proofread it for you.

Make sure your book is formatted properly and contains the front and back material organized correctly.

Take the time to put together a quality table of contents–most word processors will do this for you.

Don't forget about your book cover, your Amazon Book page, your Author Central pages, your book trailer, and everything else that goes with it. For every single book you produce, these things need to be of high quality and complete.

A poor book cover will stop your sales cold in their tracks and make you look unprofessional and amateurish. More than a handful of grammar or spelling errors will make you look sloppy and undermine your credibility. A poorly written book description can reduce your sales dramatically, and an amateurish book trailer will be ignored and not help with sales as you intended.

Keep in mind, however, that these things cost money and time. For every book, balance quality and speed of production.

Authors write books because they feel passionate about subjects, and because they want to make money. Both motivations demand that you deliver a high-quality product. Create the best product that you can within the timeframe and with the resources that you have available.

QUANTITY

By now the why should be clear, so let's focus on the income mechanic. Every book you publish stays listed indefinitely. Most earn modest amounts — a few dollars to a few hundred a month. But they stack. Thirty books each averaging $50 a month is $1,500 in baseline income before you write a word this month. Sixty books doubles that floor. This isn't passive income in the fantasy sense

— you still have to promote and stay visible — but it compounds in a way a single book never can.

The backlist is your safety net too. When a new book underperforms — and some will — the rest of the catalog keeps income flowing. One book bombing is a crisis. A catalog where one title underperforms is just a Tuesday.

Keep quality high enough that you're not embarrassed to put your name on it. Keep the routine consistent. Let the catalog build. That's the whole game.

WATCH YOUR STATISTICS

It's important to monitor your statistics. You have at your disposal the KDP dashboard, the ACX dashboard, and the Amazon affiliates dashboard. By putting all these together, you can get a good idea of how your books are doing.

Each of these dashboards differs totally from the other, and none of them really presents the information in the most useful format. KDP is the most difficult to interpret because you have the option of seeing all the statistics in summary, or each one individually.

I recommend making it a point to examine your sales statistics at the end of each day. Pick a consistent time and take a screenshot of your KDP and ACX sales statistics. This way you'll be able to compare sales from day to day. You can use these screenshots later as social proof in advertising.

It's important to track your sales on a consistent basis, either daily or weekly, because if the sales of a book dip, you'll want to know that right away, so you can investigate the reasons. It could be as simple as a promotion ending, or as complicated as someone else published a book on the same topic and category, which took away some of your own sales.

You'll also learn the pattern of your sales. For example, *Focus on LinkedIn* has better sales on the weekend than on weekdays, whereas *How to Sell on eBay* is exactly the opposite.

Higher sales could be for many reasons:

- A promotion.
- The book moved up in ranking.
- Amazon noticed it's been selling well and is promoting it.
- An external event has caused a surge in sales.
- You added it to AMS (Amazon Ads).

Reasons why sales can fall include:

- No promotion.
- A failed promotion.
- The book moved down in ranking.
- You removed the book from AMS or changed its keywords.
- Amazon removed it from a category.
- Amazon suspended the book (this will result in no sales).
- Amazon stopped promoting it.
- A competing book is taking some of the sales.
- It is a holiday (sales typically drop on a holiday).

- Some external event has occurred (such as a national disaster, a baseball game or an election).

Sometimes you can figure out why the sales of a book have changed, and sometimes it can be very obscure. What is important is that when sales drop, investigate and act keeping in mind that sometimes sales drop temporarily for some reason (such as a national emergency).

CONTINUOUS LEARNING

To stay ahead of the game, you must educate yourself and learn constantly. There are many courses available all over the web, some of them good, and some of them not so good.

I found it best to take small courses, sometimes as short as an hour, on specific topics. These courses are inexpensive, and since they're so short, I can always find time to get through them.

Udemy.com has many thousands of courses on every conceivable subject. I found the quality is good; the courses are short and straightforward, and they stick to the point.

Udemy has frequent sales, lowering the price of courses to $10 or $15 sometimes. Get on their mailing list and wait for the sales or coupons.

Continuing education is vital for you to prosper as a self-published author. I've taken literally over 100 courses in the past couple of years to learn the ins and outs of writing, self-publishing, editing, creating book covers, graphics, and dozens of other subjects related one way or another to self-publishing and writing books.

However, be on your guard because some courses offer "get rich quick" or "make zillions of dollars in less than a minute" and so forth. I've taken my fair share of these, and what I've learned from experience is that what is successful at making a living as a self-published author is walking the walk–in other words, doing the work.

AVOID THE SCAMS AND SCHEMES

In every field, there are people and businesses offering services and products. Some genuinely help. Many do not. Marketing webinars, however, are almost always marketing funnels and should be avoided at all costs. They may look attractive, but they are always carefully designed to cause you to buy products you don't need.

The usual pattern is predictable: an invitation to a free one-hour webinar that gives away one or two small tips, then funnels you into heavily packaged products and high-pressure upsells. Even when a webinar contains useful tidbits, the primary goal is to sell–your time is consumed and your attention is harvested for follow-ups that rarely deliver true long-term value.

I learned this the hard way early in my career. I ended up on dozens of lists, watched the webinars, and bought products that promised quick returns. Some purchases paid off, but most were a waste of time and money.

Here's a simple rule: skip the webinar and evaluate the product on its own merits. If you're considering a purchase, insist on the following before you hand over money:

- They must offer a no-questions-asked money-back guarantee.
- The product must be usable on its own without mandatory upsells. Upsells are fine, but the base product should deliver real value without them.
- The price must be reasonable relative to the promised value.
- Most important: will you use it, or will it sit on your hard drive collecting dust?

Avoid marketing webinars at all costs and buy only by these standards. They may look attractive, but they are always carefully designed to cause you to buy products you don't need.

ETHICS

Every career has ethical landmines. Writing is no different. A few that are worth thinking about as you build yours:

Is your book truthful? This sounds obvious, but it's easy to slip into one-sided storytelling, especially when the subject is personal. A ghostwriting client of mine wanted the book to be a takedown of everyone who'd wronged him. Since there are always multiple sides to every story, I pushed back. Your book doesn't have to be neutral, but it should be honest.

Have you done the research? Unverified claims in a nonfiction book can result in bad reviews, public embarrassment, or a lawsuit. Cite what needs citing. Paraphrase properly. Don't fake credentials you don't have.

Have you betrayed a confidence? If someone told you something in private, think carefully before putting it in print. There are cases where you need to — abuse, fraud, public danger — but most of the time it's not worth the damage it does.

Is everything actually done right? Cover, description, proofreading, title — if you rush any of these and the quality shows, that's on you. Don't publish something you'd be embarrassed to hand to a stranger.

Are you keeping the business side honest? Taxes, bookkeeping, licenses — these aren't glamorous, but ignoring them creates problems that compound. Know your numbers.

Watch out for the temptation to create something ethically questionable — pyramid schemes, slanderous content, books that promise things they can't deliver. The short money is never worth the long damage.

Simple rule: if something feels wrong, it probably is. If a deal sounds too good to be true, find the lie. Staying ethical keeps your reputation intact and your career moving in the right direction.

Write as many quality books as you can and treat royalties as your base, not your ceiling. Coaching, ghostwriting, courses, speaking, consulting—your books open those doors. Use them.

Chapter 17: It's a Business

Treat your writing career as a business. If you depend upon your income as a self-published author, then you need to take it seriously and ensure you are running it as a proper business, and not as a hobby.

BUSINESS LICENSE

Most localities require a business license to operate a home-based business. The cost is usually modest — often $25 to $75 a year — and the process is straightforward. Go to your local city or county website, search for "home occupation permit" or "business license," and follow the steps. Some areas have additional zoning requirements for home offices, particularly if clients will be visiting. Most authors working alone with no foot traffic have no issues, but check before you assume.

Don't skip this because it seems bureaucratic. Operating without a required license is the kind of small problem that becomes a big one if you ever need to prove you run a legitimate business — for a loan, a contract dispute, or a tax audit.

Local Taxes

Some cities and counties levy a local business tax on top of state and federal taxes. It's not universal, but it exists in enough places that you should check. Your city or county revenue department's website will tell you what applies. It's usually a small flat fee or a percentage of gross receipts, and the filing process is simple once you know it exists.

If you're unsure what applies to you, ask the accountant you should already have at this point. A good accountant who works with self-employed clients will know exactly what your locality requires and will make sure you're not filing late or missing obligations you didn't know about.

State and Federal Taxes

Any income you make is taxable at the state and federal levels. Keep excellent records of all your income and expenses.

A service such as QuickBooks–the self-employed version is very affordable–can be very helpful in organizing the record-keeping associated with your small business. You can use this to record all the financial details of your business. Better still, QuickBooks can read in the information from your credit cards and bank accounts and give you the opportunity to categorize that based upon personal or business expenses.

Keep in mind that being a self-published author means you are self-employed–even if you or full-time employed at another job. This means you can write off expenses such as part of your home is a home office, health insurance premiums, communications, and part of your car, among other things. It's best to go over this with an accountant, who will fill you in on what you can and can't write off.

If you publish through Amazon–KDP or ACX–you'll receive the tax forms from them at the end of the year. They will also report all your income to the IRS (or the equivalent for other countries) and other government agencies as required.

HOME OFFICE

If you work from home — and as a self-published author, you almost certainly do — you can deduct a portion of your housing costs as a business expense. The IRS allows this under the home office deduction, but only if the space is used regularly and exclusively for business. A dedicated room is ideal. A corner of your bedroom where you also watch TV doesn't qualify.

The deduction is calculated as a percentage of your home's square footage. If your office takes up 10% of your home, you can deduct 10% of your rent or mortgage interest, utilities, internet, and other housing costs. There's also a simplified method — $5 per square foot of office space, up to 300 square feet — which is easier to calculate and audit-proof. Talk to your accountant about which method makes more sense for your situation.

Set up the office properly. Get a good desk, a chair that won't destroy your back over years of sitting, and whatever else you need to work effectively. The money you spend setting up a functional workspace is itself deductible, and working in a comfortable, dedicated space makes you more productive. Both things are true.

Almost everything you spend money on for your writing business is deductible. Computer equipment, software subscriptions, writing courses, books related to your work, cover design fees, editing costs, hosting fees, domain registrations, printing, postage, office supplies, professional memberships — all of it.

The key is documentation. Keep every receipt, every invoice, every confirmation email. I keep a folder for each tax year and drop everything in there as it happens. Come tax time, everything is in one place. QuickBooks Self-Employed is worth the subscription — it connects to your bank and credit card accounts and lets you categorize transactions quickly. At the end of the year, exporting the data for your accountant takes minutes instead of days.

Large equipment purchases — a computer, a camera, an external hard drive setup — may need to be depreciated over several years rather than deducted all at once, depending on the amount and how your taxes are structured. Your accountant handles this. The point is: spend the money you need to spend on your business, track it, and deduct it. Running your business on the cheap just to avoid spending money you'll get back at tax time is penny-wise and pound-foolish.

WORKING HOURS

Figure out when your brain works and protect those hours. I'm ADHD and my schedule reflects that — I work from 4 a.m. to 11 a.m., take a long break, then go again from 4 p.m. to midnight. That's when I'm productive. Build your schedule around how your brain actually operates, not what a normal workday is supposed to look like.

Your schedule doesn't need to look like mine. What matters is that you define it, protect it, and get enough sleep. Self-employment makes it easy to drift into working at all hours and burning out quietly. Set the hours, tell the people around you what they are, and stick to them.

BACKUPS

Back up everything, in multiple places, on a regular schedule. Losing a manuscript to a crashed drive is not a hypothetical — it happens, and it's devastating.

My setup uses three layers. Backblaze runs continuously and sends everything offsite — if my machine is stolen or destroyed, my files are safe. On top of that I do disk-to-disk backups: a weekly backup to one external drive and a monthly backup to a separate drive stored elsewhere. That way a single event can't take out everything at once.

Three layers sounds like overkill until it isn't. Cloud backup alone fails if your account is compromised. Local drives fail if there's a fire or theft. All three together means you can recover from almost anything without losing more than a few hours of work.

SAVE OFTEN

Save constantly. I hit save every few paragraphs — it's muscle memory. Set Word to auto-save every five to ten minutes as a backstop. If your system crashes mid-chapter you want to lose five minutes of work, not two hours.

Also save to a second location as you go. Configure Word to save to a Dropbox, Google Drive, or OneDrive folder so every save also syncs offsite automatically. Thirty seconds to set up, never think about it again until the day it saves you.

DON'T SKIMP ON WHAT IS IMPORTANT

Money is always an issue for every business, and it's important to know where money should be spent and where it can be saved. Don't be a person who is penny wise and pound foolish. What this means is don't be one of those people who say that penny here and there while costing themselves real money in lost profits or opportunities.

Where should you spend your money?

- Spend the money to purchase good web hosting. I recommend SiteGround because their hosting is rock solid, stable, performs well, and their support is excellent. For just a few dollars a month, probably less than a single cup of Starbucks coffee, you'll get a professional hosting service. This also comes with a free domain name (the first year) which you'll need to establish your brand.
- Hire a local professional to take photos for your author biography and media kits.
- Hire a local professional designer to work with you to create a logo to establish your brand.

- Invest in a good computer for your word-processing needs. As a professional writer, you'll spend a good portion of typing on your computer every day, so you want to make sure you have one that is reliable and fast.
- Investment a good chair to be nice to your back. Much of your day will be spent sitting in front of your computer, which can be hell on your back.
- Spend the money to join organizations, as described in Writing Associations, to network with other writers in your area. This can be of immense help in furthering your writing career as you can find beta readers, people who will critique your work, proofreaders, and other specialties that you'll need.
- Invest in training either online or at your local community college to further your mind and skills.
- Work with good outsources to proofread your work, design, and create book covers and so forth.

CONTROL EXPENSES

Keep unnecessary expenses under control. While it is important to know what is required for your business, it's equally important to understand what isn't needed.

Resist the "shiny object syndrome." As you proceed through your writing career, and research on the Internet, you'll find many "money making" offers of all types. You'll see advertisements for training applications on how to create and sell puzzle books, coloring books, comic books, calendars, and just about anything else you can think of.

While some of these are completely valid and may help you make some money, the best strategy is to find your niche (or niches) and focus on that area instead of going for the quick buck and something that sounds fantastic in an advertisement or webinar.

Personally, I've spent more than I like to think about on shiny objects that I thought might help my writing career or short-circuit some of the work needed to make money in this field.

I can tell you from experience, just focus your attention on your goals and your niche, and be willing to change direction if that's not working out or if needed.

INCORPORATING

I'm not incorporated. For many self-publishing authors starting out, a sole proprietorship is fine — simpler taxes, less paperwork, no annual fees. As your income grows, it's worth a conversation with an accountant about whether an LLC or S-corp makes sense. The main reasons to incorporate are liability protection and potential tax advantages once you're earning enough that the structure pays for itself. Don't incorporate because it sounds professional. Do it when the numbers justify it.

CONCLUSIONS

Are you planning to make a career out of being a self-published author?

If you answered yes, then ensure you treat it as a business. As soon as you decide it is or is going to be your career, you've also created a business.

Treat it like one.

Chapter 18: Conclusions

You can make a living; in fact, you can make a good living as a self-published author. Treat it the same as you would any other career–it's going to take education, training, practice, hard work, and networking with other like-minded professionals.

Where should you begin? Write your first book quickly while maintaining high quality. Set aside at least four hours every day, more if possible, or you can sequester yourself away from others and write your book. Yes, of course, do research to determine if there's a market for the book, but don't overthink it.

You see, that first book, getting it written and published, is a huge milestone for a self-published author. It means you are successful! You've accomplished something that very few have done–you've written and published a book.

Don't get discouraged if your first book doesn't sell; oh, you'll sell a few copies to friends, family members, coworkers, and others that you know, but very few first books sell more than a few dozen or a few hundred copies.

While you're writing that first book, start working on your author brand and platform. Create a blog and email list and choose which social media is best for you.

Well before you publish, begin writing short, 300-word or so articles for your blog and social media about your book. You could take a paragraph from one chapter, put it in quotes, and write a couple of paragraphs about what it means. Mention that this is from your up-and-coming book.

If you're feeling daring, make a video of yourself talking about your book. You can even have a friend interview you, if you want. Explain why you wrote it, what benefits it has for your readers, why you decided to become an author, and so forth. Remember to include the name of your blog and your book in the interview.

Post that video to YouTube and share it around your social media.

This will get you used to working with social media and building a buzz, as it's called, about the book you'll be publishing soon. More than likely, others in your friend list and groups will comment on these posts, which will enable you to give even more information.

Once your book is published, spend some time letting your friends, families, coworkers and other people know that you've written it and that it is now for sale on Amazon.

Then get started on your next book and use the lessons that you've learned from the first book to make the second book even better.

Continue this process until you have built a respectable blog with several dozen or more articles, you have over 50 people on your email list, and you've been posting regularly to the social media of your choice.

Don't even think about purchasing any advertising, buying banner ads, or spending any money on promotion at all until your blog, author platform, email list, Amazon Author Central, and the other things talked about in this book are mature.

By that I mean that you have gained a following of people who are interested in what you have to say and want to read what you publish.

You might be ready to do this after your first book, your second, or may even take half a dozen. In my case, I purchased paid advertising right away and wasted a lot of money. In hindsight, my author platform and related materials were not mature until I had completed a dozen books.

The most important thing is to keep at it. Continue to write books, publish them, and work your blog, email list, and social media. Keep communicating with your readers and continue to build your network of authors and other like-minded professionals.

Don't let anybody get in your way — you can make it if you put in the effort, get the education, and do the right things.

One last thought. This book returns to the same idea in almost every chapter: publish more good books. By now you understand why that's not a productivity slogan — it's the structure of the business. Research gets you books worth writing. Routine gets them written. Quality gets them reviewed. Platform gets them found. Metadata gets them ranked. The catalog compounds. Every element of this book is in service of that one outcome — a body of work that earns while you write the next one.

Start the first book. Finish it. Publish it. Then write the next one.

One author I interviewed said something worth ending on. This path is not meant for everybody. It's going to be difficult. There will be times when you feel like you're walking alone. That's fine — it happens to all of us. Sit down deep within yourself and decide whether this is what you really want. Not because it's easy, not because the money is guaranteed, but because you have something to say and you want to say it. Then commit to it and go forward without regrets.

Books by Richard Lowe

See books by Richard Lowe at

https://masterofworlds.com

Get free publishing insights and industry updates at

https://thewritingking.substack.com

For ghostwriting and book coaching services see

https://thewritingking.com